*God's Pathway
to Healing*

VITAMINS AND
SUPPLEMENTS

BOOKS BY
REGINALD B. CHERRY, M.D.

GOD'S PATHWAY TO HEALING:

Bone Health

Diabetes

Digestion

Heart

Herbs That Heal

Joints and Arthritis

The Immune System

Memory and Mental Acuity

Menopause

Prostate

Vision

Vitamins and Supplements

Dr. Cherry's Little Instruction Book

03C

God's Pathway
to Healing

VITAMINS AND
SUPPLEMENTS

by

Reginald B. Cherry, M.D.

BETHANYHOUSE
Minneapolis, Minnesota

God's Pathway to Healing: Vitamins and Supplements
Copyright © 2003
Reginald B. Cherry, M.D.

Manuscript prepared by Rick Killian, Killian Creative,
Boulder, Colorado. *www.killiancreative.com*

Cover design by Danielle White

Note: The directions given in this book are in no way to be
considered a substitute for consultation with your own
physician.

Italics in Scripture quotes denote author emphasis.

Unless otherwise indicated, scripture quotations are from the
King James Version of the Bible.

Scripture quotations identified AMP are from *The Amplified
Bible* copyright © 1965 by the Zondervan Corporation. Used
by permission.

Published by Bethany House Publishers
11400 Hampshire Avenue South
Bloomington, Minnesota 55438

Bethany House Publishers is a Division of
Baker Book House Company, Grand Rapids, Michigan.

Printed in the United States of America

ISBN 0-7642-2813-7

CONTENTS

INDEX OF CHARTS

INTRODUCTION

The medical community is at a major turning point on the subject of vitamins and supplements. For years doctors have told their patients that they could get all the vitamins, minerals, and nutrients they needed from the food they ate. Yet the depletions in the soil and environment, as well as an American diet that has radically turned toward fast and fatty processed foods, have made them begin to change their minds. General sub-par levels of vitamins are being noted in most Americans, and these deficiencies are beginning to be linked more and more with chronic illness and disease. Low omega-3 fatty acid levels are being linked with heart disease, Alzheimer's, and other problems. Time and time again sickness is being linked with not getting the nutrition needed from our foods. For these reasons, for the first time, members of the medical community are starting to recommend that patients take vitamins and supplements on a daily basis.

When "supplements" are mentioned, people tend to get a lot of different ideas because the technology of "multivitamins" has changed so dramatically in the last couple of decades. We used to refer to them as "vitamin supplements," then as "vitamin and mineral supplements." A little later they became "high-potency vitamin and mineral supplements." Today, however, modern technology has taken us far beyond simply having vitamins and minerals in tablet form. In fact, we now refer to "nutritional supplements," because what is available to us goes beyond vitamins and minerals to include fruit, vegetable, and plant extracts as well as various enzymes. Meanwhile, more and more research is showing the benefits these have for us if we keep a constant level of them in our bloodstream.

Because of changing technology and the

increase in research showing the benefits of taking certain elements on a daily basis, opinions, advice, and products now abound telling us what we need to stay healthy. As a result, our ministry has received many letters from those who have found themselves spending as much as $100 to $150 a month to get everything they have been told "is essential for a basic nutritional supplement program," while others are more confused than ever trying to figure out how to take all of the different supplements they have been told they need. Others have been shocked to find they were ingesting potentially harmful dosages of some compounds as a result of receiving the same elements from too many different sources. With all of this cost and confusion, as well as a lot of advice that is based more on selling a product than on truly helping people find what they need, how can we know what to take and what not to take for our daily nutritional needs?

Well, I want you to know that my wife, Linda, and I have made this journey ourselves.

We have gone from the bottles—up to twenty-five at one point—to the fly-fisherman's box with its eighteen compartments in which we stored our daily regimen of pills, capsules, and tablets. I will never forget the chaos that emerged from having dropped the box; we had to throw out the entire lot and start over. Some things we found we were getting too much of due to their replication in various products. Yet over the years, through my practice and through reading hundreds and hundreds of research articles, we have been able to work it down to a set of elements that can be taken easily on a daily basis, giving us the nutritional protection we need. We have also found in our research that the additional supplementation of certain vitamins, minerals, extracts, or enzymes can help if you are facing specific health issues.

In Matthew 24, Jesus said that we would face "pestilences" in the last days that would be the beginning of great sorrow but also that those who endure to the end shall be saved. God is preparing His people who are facing diseases and pollutants in their environment in order that they can endure to the end, because He also promised that we would be satisfied with long life and be shown His salvation. (See Psalm 91:16.) This preparation is both spiritual and physical. Just as there are things that we do daily to strengthen our spirits to resist physical temptation, there are things we should do to strengthen our bodies in order to resist physical illness and disease. More than being healed, God wants us to walk in constant divine health. It is my belief that nutritional supplements are a key to God's plan for healthy living and that He will lead us in finding the supplements that are right for us so that we can walk in strength and fulfill His plan for our lives in these last days.

—Reginald B. Cherry, M.D.

Chapter 1

GOD'S BEST IS THAT WE LIVE WITHOUT DISEASE

Chapter 1

GOD'S BEST IS THAT WE LIVE WITHOUT DISEASE

"Ye shall serve the LORD your God, and he shall bless thy bread, and thy water; and *I will take sickness away from the midst of thee*. There shall nothing cast their young, nor be barren, in thy land: *the number of thy days I will fulfill*" (Exodus 23:25–26).

It was never God's plan that His people live with sickness and disease. From the beginning God put healing power within us in the form of our immune system, for example, and put the plants and other foods on the earth that would nourish that system so that it could keep illness away from us. I also believe it is this system that God spoke of in Exodus 23 when He told Israel that he would "take sickness away from the midst of [them]" and "the number of [their] days [he would] fulfill."

God gave a precursor to these two promises, though, in verse 25. First, God would bless their food and their water. A great health benefit would be found in the foods they ate. The fact is that modern science is now finding that the foods they ate in Bible times are what we have come to call the Mediterranean diet, and it is perhaps the healthiest diet available on earth. These promises of God are linked to the nutrients we get from the foods we eat. These nutrients feed and strengthen our body's systems, but it is incredible how crucial they are to the proper functioning of our immune system. An essential key to a full, long life is a strong, healthy immune system.

Some Christians think this emphasis on watching what we eat is unnecessary because it is not spiritual. They might say something like, "If God really wants us healthy, can't He supernaturally protect us with a resistance to disease and illness?" The answer is that He could, but that is not the way He designed us, nor is it the way He operates. Let me put this in another light for clarification.

A parallel question might be, "If God doesn't want us to sin, than couldn't He simply keep us from sinning?" Again, the answer is that He could, but then we would have no free will. Instead, He chose to give us His Word so that we could learn about His forgiveness and salvation through Jesus' death on the cross, His resurrection, and His ascension. He also outlined in His Word how we might walk in His holiness and righteousness and be His representatives on the earth. These are not things we automatically walk in when we become Christians, but they are things we need to study in the Bible so that we can learn to apply them to our daily lives; otherwise, the holiness and righteousness Jesus won for us through the cross would have no way of being manifest in our lives. The key to experiencing them is living the way the Bible tells us to live.

Is walking in divine health any different? We may think it is obvious that we cannot violate God's spiritual laws and walk in righteousness at the same time; why then do we find it so hard to believe that we can violate God's dietary laws (e.g., not eating fat as outlined in Leviticus 3:17 and 7:23) and still walk in divine health? God's plan was that we would find the nutrients our bodies need to keep strong and healthy in the foods we ate. This was the purpose of the dietary laws God gave His people—it was His way of blessing their bread and water.

Medical science is now confirming these laws as good guidelines for what we do and do not eat. For example, studies have found that dropping a diet high in fat can dramatically increase the number and function of NK (natural killer) cells in our immune systems (these are the cells that seek out and destroy bacteria, viruses, and cancer-causing agents— they are the frontline cells of the immune system).[1] God's dietary laws were designed for our health.

Now, I don't mean to turn this into a form of legalism and bondage as to what you can and cannot eat. Paul warned us about systems that try to control us even to the point of what we eat—"touch not, taste not"—in Colossians chapter 2, but what I am trying to say is that in His creation God gave us most of the things we need to stay healthy, and His Word tells us of many of them. More often than not these natural foods and practices are better than anything that can be found in pharmaceutical medications. God's plan was that our bodies would remain strong and be able to fight off disease through the nutrients we received daily in the foods we ate.

Medical science is now confirming this in study after study. The field of nutrition is exploding as we are finding more and more about helping people stay healthy by eating the right things and avoiding the wrong things. I have seen more articles in the past year about vitamins and supplements than I have in the preceding ten years in medical journals. The research and interest in this topic is at the highest level I have ever seen.

Because of this emphasis on getting the right nutrients into our bodies, the industry of vitamin and mineral supplements has also exploded in recent years, as have health-food stores. Roughly 6.6 million dollars *a day* are spent on vitamins. Confusion is also rampant because there are so many differing opinions, and people don't know what the appropriate dosages are. Yet in response to the many alternatives and questions from their patients about what kind of supplements they should take, doctors have always emphasized that we can get all the vitamins, minerals, and other nutrients our bodies need through the foods we eat. This has always been the case; that is, until recently.

For the first time the medical community is pronouncing that our diet is not enough and that daily supplements of one form or another are becoming increasingly necessary. I believe there are a couple of reasons for this.

One is that our foods are being depleted of their nutrients because modern farming and breeding techniques emphasize quantity and not quality (I will discuss this in more detail in chapter 2). I also believe this is because we are confronted with diseases today that have never before been faced in the history of the world. Jesus told us that in the end times "there will be … in various places famines and pestilences (plagues, malignant and contagious or infectious epidemic diseases, deadly and devastating). And there will be sights of terror and great signs from the heavens" (Luke 21:11 AMP). I believe Jesus is talking about the age in which we are now living and about the great famines and pestilences that are on the earth today.

It is all too common that we hear of new viruses, such as the West Nile virus, or ones that are yet to be named and which doctors don't know how to treat. Cancer is on the rise. Statistics show that half of Americans will die of heart disease. There are also infections against which antibiotics can no longer be effective. Tuberculosis is on the increase again after declining for thirty-two straight years. The World Health Organization estimates that there are 8 million new cases of tuberculosis across the world each year while 20 million people currently suffer its devastating symptoms. AIDS, a disease no one had even heard of three decades ago, is decimating whole nations. Another issue is air pollution—most of us breathe it in every day. Who knows what the long-term effect of that will be? And this is just the tip of the iceberg; if these things don't fulfill what Jesus was describing in Luke 21, I don't know what could.

Jesus didn't tell us about these things to put fear in our hearts; He was warning us so that we could prepare ourselves. Just before He mentioned these signs, He said, "Be on your guard and be careful that you are not led astray" (Luke 21:8 AMP). In other words, He was instructing us so that when we encountered these things, we would know how to respond and counteract them. If we are open to His Spirit, He will lead us down the pathway to divine health.

God designed our immune system to be our basic defense mechanism against disease. What we are seeing in many of the cases I just mentioned is a failure of that system. AIDS, for example, is a direct attack on the immune system and is a large reason for the increase in tuberculosis. It is a failure of the immune system that leads to cancer. The rampant spread of bacterial infections and new viruses is also because of a general reduction in the effectiveness of our immune system. Our immune systems are weak and unable to combat these things because they are not getting the nutrients they need or are overstressed because we are eating the wrong things.

This is why I feel that the issue of vitamins and supplements is so critical. I believe it is also the reason behind the medical community's change in its stance toward taking daily nutritional supplements.

Now that you understand part of God's natural plan for your health, it is time to take a more in-depth look at what medical research is now saying about vitamins and supplements and begin to start clearing up the confusion about what to take and what not to take in the area of vitamins, minerals, extracts, and enzymes.

God's best is that we walk in health all the days of our lives. If we are open to Him, the Holy Spirit will show us the things we need to do to walk on this path toward divine health and the role nutritional supplements should play for us whether we are healthy at the moment or need to address certain health issues. God's plan for healthy living has always combined what we can do in the natural with what God can do in the supernatural, so let's begin to see what we can start to do today to embark on this pathway to health and healing.

Chapter 2

MEDICAL SCIENCE IS CHANGING ITS MIND ABOUT VITAMINS AND SUPPLEMENTS

Chapter 2

MEDICAL SCIENCE IS CHANGING ITS MIND ABOUT VITAMINS AND SUPPLEMENTS

As we have said, it has long been the mantra of the medical community that we can get all the vitamins and nutrients we need from the food we eat every day. This belief has also included a traditional food pyramid of four basic food groups: (1) breads and cereals as the base; (2) fruits and vegetables next up; (3) then dairy two or three times a day; and (4) two or three servings a day of meat and proteins; and atop those four, fats, oils, and sweets used sparingly. This mindset, however, is dramatically changing.

Recent articles appearing in both *Scientific American* and *Newsweek* have cited the switch from this "Four Basic Food Groups" pyramid to a new food pyramid that looks surprisingly like the Mediterranean diet we have been recommending in our ministry for some time. This new pyramid has daily exercise and weight control at its base; with whole grain foods and plant oil—olive, canola, soy, corn, sunflower, peanut, etc.—at the next level (suggesting these are eaten at most meals); followed by fruits and vegetables (five to nine servings a day); nuts and legumes or beans (one to three servings a day); fish, poultry, and eggs (zero to two servings a day); dairy or calcium supplement (once or twice a day); and red meat, butter, white rice, white bread, potatoes, pasta, and sweets at the top (eaten sparingly).[1] This switch in the food pyramid is just part of the new emphasis on nutrition for prevention that is occurring in the medical community.

Yet more remarkable than the changes in the food pyramid are the changes doctors are making with respect to vitamins and supplements. It has only been recently that publications such as *The Journal of the American Medical Association* (*JAMA*) and organizations such as the American Heart Association (AHA) have come out plainly stating that supplements should be part of our everyday nutritional program in addition to the foods we eat.

A study related in the June 19, 2002, issue of *JAMA* plainly states, "We recommend that all adults take one multivitamin daily." The main reasons that the authors cited this were the documented benefits they saw from the regular intake of folate as well as vitamins B_{12}, B_6, and D in the prevention of cardiovascular disease, cancer, and osteoporosis. They also cited that most multivitamins have safe dosages of these needed nutrients and are relatively inexpensive. They also recommended two multivitamins daily for older people, although they cautioned that taking too much vitamin A can lead to hip fractures, and too much iron can increase the risk of hemochromatosis that some face. Despite these risks, they suggested daily multivitamin intake because of the simplicity of taking them regularly and the general suboptimal levels of most vitamins for the general population in the United States.[2]

Alongside this, the American Heart Association has also recently announced that it recommends patients with documented cases of coronary heart disease take a daily supplement of 1 gram of omega-3 fatty acids every day. This is recommended due to the difficulty of getting adequate amounts of omega-3's through diet alone. Three ounces of fatty fish such as salmon, herring, trout, or sardines every day would provide the same benefits, but it is not always possible, economical, or desirable to eat this much fish so often. Noting that eating fish on a regular basis is not easily done, they have suggested the fatty acid capsule as a reasonable and effective alternative. The eicosapentaenoic acid (EPA) and the docosahexaenoic acid (DHA) found in these fish oils have been shown in clinical trials to reduce the incidence of new coronary heart disease events in patients who are known to already have the disease. The article announcing this also stated that this is the first pill supplement ever recommended by the AHA.[3]

These changes are coming because there has been so much research showing the benefits of certain supplements in recent years. Large organizations such as the American Medical Association and the American Heart Association take a long time to review all of these materials, discuss them among their various members and committees, and then come to a consensus as to how to act in response to the findings of these studies. Organizations such as our ministry can often move much faster in bringing such recommendations to the public, which is why we started suggesting vitamin and mineral supplementation years ago and more recently added enzyme and extract supplements (one of which is a fish oil capsule) to what we recommend people take every day. It is my belief that the medical community will soon catch up to these recommendations for a daily nutritional supplement program.

I personally believe that one of the simplest steps we need to consider to maintain our health in these last days is to take nutritional supplements on a daily basis. You should pray about this and discuss taking supplements with your doctor at your routine checkup. The question is no longer whether or not you should be on a program but rather what should be included in your nutritional supplement program to best protect yourself in the world in which we live today.

Although the medical community in general does not yet recommend a specific program of supplements, study after study is coming out on the benefits of multivitamins and supplements for strengthening our body's ability to fight off sickness and disease. In one study at Memorial University of Newfoundland, they found that patients on a daily supplement that had eighteen different ingredients—a combination of vitamins, minerals, trace elements, and so on—had an increase in short-term memory and an increase in immune function. This research was on a group of healthy, independent men and women over the age of sixty-five.[4] At the University of Iowa they found that nutritional deficiencies significantly increase as we age and that regularly taking supplements can eliminate these deficiencies.[5] Another study reported in the *American Journal of Clinical Nutrition* showed that multivitamin and mineral supplements taken daily can boost lymphocyte and immune system function.[6] In another study from Germany done on adult men and women who suffered from stress and exhaustion, taking a daily multivitamin with probiotics at breakfast reduced their stress levels by just over 40 percent. Probiotics are the good bacteria in the colon that research has found can affect the immune system. In addition to the drop in stress, they showed a 29 percent decrease in the frequency of infections and a 91 percent drop in gastrointestinal discomforts, two problems highly associated with stress.[7]

WE ARE NOT GETTING THE VITAMINS AND NUTRIENTS OUR BODIES NEED

Although vitamin deficiency syndromes such as scurvy and beriberi are extremely uncommon today, medical science has long noted that people in general, and especially the elderly, do not get the full recommended dosages of vitamins that they need. This suboptimal level of vitamin intake and absorption is strongly linked to the risk of chronic diseases. Sub-par levels of folic acid and vitamins B_6 and B_{12} are risk factors for cardiovascular disease, neural tube damage, and colon or breast cancer. Did you know that heart disease kills more people than all the forms of cancer combined? It is true. Low levels of vitamin D contribute to osteopenia (bone thinning) and bone fractures, while suboptimal levels of the antioxidant vitamins (vitamins A, E, and C) can increase the risk for several chronic diseases.[8]

This general suboptimal level of dietary vitamins is something to which we should all pay attention because of the risks associated with low vitamin levels. The following chart outlines some of the things to watch for when considering your level of vitamin intake.

Signs of Vitamin Deficiency[9]	
Vitamin A (beta carotene)	Night blindness; abnormal dryness in the eyes; dry, rough, itchy skin; susceptibility to respiratory infection
Vitamin B$_1$ (thiamine)	Confusion; weakness of eye muscles; loss of appetite; uncoordinated walk; poor memory; inability to concentrate
Vitamin B$_2$ (riboflavin)	Discolored tongue; anemia; cracks at the corners of the mouth; scaly skin; burning, itchy eyes
Vitamin B$_3$ (niacin)	Insomnia; headache; diarrhea; dementia; dermatitis (inflammation of the skin)
Vitamin B$_6$ (pyridoxine)	Depression; skin lesions; extreme nervousness; water retention; lethargy

Vitamin B$_{12}$ (cobalamin)	Anemia accompanied by symptoms such as heart palpitations, sore tongue, or general weakness; weight loss
Folic Acid	Anemia; dizziness; fatigue; intestinal disorders; diarrhea; shortness of breath
Vitamin C (ascorbic acid)	Easy bruising; spongy, bleeding gums; dental problems; slow wound healing; fatigue; listlessness; rough skin
Vitamin D (cholecalciferol)	Softening of bones; bone pain; susceptibility to bone fracture; excessive tooth decay
Vitamin E (tocopherol)	Muscle degeneration; anemia; nerve dysfunction

OUR FOODS DON'T CONTAIN THE NUTRIENTS THEY USED TO CONTAIN

While no one can deny that the foundation to our health is in the foods we eat—and don't eat—it must also be noted that the nutritional value of our food is not what it used to be. To begin with, many of us, to save time and energy, have turned to highly refined, prepackaged convenience foods. In general these refined foods contain up to 80 percent fewer vital nutrients than do whole or natural foods.

And then, even if we do manage to eat primarily unprocessed foods, here are some other interesting statistics to consider when talking about our vitamin and mineral intake through diet. There was recently a study done comparing statistics from 1936 about various trace minerals and micronutrients in foods we normally eat with levels in those same foods today. They found the following changes in the average nutrient levels of these foods:

- Calcium levels have dropped 24 percent.
- Magnesium levels have dropped 28 percent.
- Potassium levels are down 10 percent.
- Iron is down 22 percent.
- Copper is down 81 percent.

The reason for this is the desire to grow greater numbers of high-yield plants to maximize harvests (and profits), but in general we are not as concerned with the nutritional value of the fruits and vegetables produced. The trend is toward bigger chickens, bigger cows, and bigger livestock in general but not necessarily more nutritional value in the food products taken from these animals. Fertilizers are used containing such things as nitrogen and phosphorus, which help to grow big, high-yield crops but which actually decrease the nutritional value of those crops. We have deserted the more natural, organic methods of farming for the sake of growing plants whose leaves and stalks are huge and animals that weigh more but whose trace minerals and nutritional values are significantly lower.

Here's another survey I came across in the research that has turned up recently. Eighty percent of our population is deficient to some degree in chromium. Chromium is a trace mineral that is also extremely lacking in our diets because our foods are so highly processed. One of its most important functions is that it helps insulin work properly in our bodies. Diabetes can develop if muscle and fat cells use insulin poorly. Did you know there are approximately 2,000 new cases of diabetes diagnosed every day? Not every month, not every year, but *every single day*. There are 16 million people estimated to have diabetes, and only one in three know it. Another 13 million people have pre-diabetes. In other words, it's just a matter of time before they develop the actual disease.

Population studies also show some dramatic decreases in zinc levels. Roughly 75 percent of us do not get the recommended daily allowance of zinc. Zinc is one of the key elements in protecting the immune system. If your immune system weakens, you are vulnerable to everything from allergies to cancer and infections, because the immune system is the vigilant guard that God has placed in us to protect our bodies from the illnesses and diseases present in the world around us.

WE NEED TO SUPPLEMENT OUR DIET TO GET THE NUTRIENTS WE NEED

Considering these lower nutritional values in our foods and the general population's sub-par levels of certain key vitamins and minerals, we find that in order to get the same benefits from the food we eat as our parents, grandparents, or great-grandparents did, we need to consume more than they did! Eating more of the right things can be complicated in our hectic schedules today. As it is, it is difficult to consume the five to nine servings of fruit and vegetables every day that are suggested by the new food pyramid. To have the right levels of the essential fatty acids in our diets we would have to add fish to our regular meals almost daily. Now, obviously this could be done, but not everyone wants to eat fish every day, and in many parts of the country having fish on such a regular basis is not very economical or convenient. We also face a pollution problem because many fish store up mercury in their systems, and if we eat them regularly, we risk dangerous levels of this poison in our own systems. Getting these marine oils in supplement form, however, is both simpler and safe.

In addition to mercury, there are toxins

and pollutants in our air and water, stress at home and in the workplace, and the ever-increasing use of pharmaceutical drugs—all of which deplete vital nutrients from our bodies. When taking all of these factors into consideration, it is easy to see why we are failing to meet our nutritional needs by relying on diet alone.

I believe that it is because of these difficulties that God has given medical science the knowledge of how to create and conveniently package nutritional supplements. He did it to make it easier for everyone to get the nutrients they need to stay healthy. With the technology available, it is also amazing how many different ailments can be addressed by starting a regular routine of taking nutritional supplements daily with our meals.

A Basic Nutritional Supplement Program Can Address Twenty-Two Different Health Concerns

As I have been studying the relationship of supplements to the prevention of disease, and even its reversal, an interesting pattern has emerged. Research indicates that there are twenty-two major diseases or health risks that can be addressed with a nutritional supplement program. The following chart records these twenty-two categories.

The Twenty-Two Major Health Categories

1. Immune Function
2. Free Radical Defense
3. Energy and Endurance
4. Joints and Muscles
5. Vision and Macular Function
6. Memory and Mental Clarity
7. Heart and Cardiovascular Function
8. Cholesterol and Triglyceride Levels
9. Blood Pressure Levels
10. Veins, Arteries, and Circulation
11. Blood Sugar Levels
12. Prostate / Men's Well-Being
13. Menopause / Women's Well-Being
14. Cellular Function
15. Weight Management
16. Mood

17. Digestion and Absorption
18. Liver and Detoxification
19. Skin, Hair, and Nails
20. Teeth and Gums
21. Lungs and Respiratory Function
22. Thyroid Function

I believe balance in each of these categories is essential to living a full, healthy life. The amazing thing is, though, that all of these twenty-two major health concerns can be addressed with just seven essential complexes or classes of supplements. The number *seven* in the Bible represents perfection. Isn't it amazing that the number of complexes we need to feed our bodies and keep them healthy is seven? Any nutritional supplement program that you take regularly should include these seven basic complexes.

TAKING SUPPLEMENTS THE EASY WAY

My wife, Linda, and I know from experience that the whole arena regarding what to take in our daily supplement program can be confusing. You hear so many claims and opinions about what you should and shouldn't take that many times you don't know what to believe.

There are so many beneficial ingredients that it can be a major challenge just to keep all of the bottles organized! As I mentioned in the introduction, when Linda and I first started our quest for the right blend of daily supplements, we went through all of this. One of the most common questions we get in this area is "What do you take every day?" Well, we started out with just a few bottles of various supplements, but gradually that became more complicated. We got to the point where we were juggling so many bottles we couldn't keep them straight. Imagine the complication of counting out all those capsules and tablets in the midst of trying to get ready for the day, trying to remember which ones you'd already taken and which you hadn't, and then getting them all down before you fly out the door to work. At one point we were dealing with twenty-five bottles of different supplements! It was crazy.

Then there was also the possibility of poisoning our systems by getting too much of some elements from the various sources. While some things, like vitamin C, are water-soluble and any excess will wash out of your system, others can build up and cause problems. For example, too much vitamin A (fat-soluble) over time can cause brittleness in your bones, while too much peppermint oil extract can cause acid reflux. Then, every time you hear of something new you should be taking, you wonder, "Is it compatible with what I am already taking?" When people take in four or five hundred different bioflavonoids every day from the fruits and vegetables they eat, plus the supplements they are already taking, there is a concern that something will cancel out the effects of others. There are over two hundred plants that contain phytoestrogen (natural plant estrogen) and so many different phyto-chemicals. There is a deficiency of iron and zinc in this country, but when they are taken in the wrong proportion, they cancel out the absorption of each other, so it is the same as taking neither. There is legitimate concern about how they all work together and about the amounts of each compound in each supplement you take and how they are formulated. You have to find well-researched advice to follow. Then you must find a way to keep everything organized and take only what you need every day. It took us a long time to figure it all out.

Then Linda had the ingenious idea to buy fly fisherman's tackle boxes that had eighteen compartments. I was really amazed at that; my scientific brain would never have thought of such a simple solution. Then every few weeks or so she would sit down at the kitchen table with our twenty-five bottles of supplements, spread them all out, count them, and organize them into the fly box compartments. Then I would carry mine with me to work to take with my lunchtime meal.

I will never forget the time I dropped my box while it was open and scattered the contents across the floor! It was quite a sight: all of these different colors and shapes spread all over. I had no idea which was which or where each should go. In the end I had to throw the whole lot out to keep from taking the wrong combination and getting too high a dose of certain things.

But I have good news for you. God has given us "knowledge of witty inventions" (Proverbs 8:12) and specifically knowledge of new nutritional supplements. He has also given us the wisdom to simplify the process of taking these supplements. Our God is not a god of confusion and did not give us a spirit of fear or confusion, but of power, love, and a sound mind. (See 1 Corinthians 14:33 and 2 Timothy 1:7.)

The key is to find or develop a system of supplements that includes these seven essential complexes to get the basic daily nutrition you need. God really does want it to be easy for you. This is why I have included a complete list of these seven complexes and their sixty-three different groups of vitamins, minerals, flavonoids, fruit and vegetable extracts, marine lipid extracts, enzymes, and other complexes that will help protect you from the twenty-two major health concerns that face us today.

The following chapter will follow that up with a discussion of these and other nutrients that can help you if you are specifically facing any of these twenty-two health challenges.

As the research has long proven—and the medical community is now starting to endorse—daily nutritional supplements are crucial to maintaining our health in these last days. As you read the following chapters, please prayerfully consider and discuss with your physician which basic nutrients are right for you and what the best way will be for you to get them into your body on a daily basis so that you can take advantage of God's plan for healthy living.

Chapter 3

THE SEVEN ESSENTIAL COMPLEXES FOR DAILY NUTRITION

Chapter 3

THE SEVEN ESSENTIAL COMPLEXES FOR DAILY NUTRITION

Would you do something simple if you knew it would help you keep healthy? I believe you would. Yes, we should all be eating more fruits and vegetables daily. We should be exercising thirty to forty-five minutes, three or four days a week. We also should watch our weight—in fact, most of us need to shed a few pounds. These are all things we should do, but they are not always easy. Let's start with the easiest thing first, then work our way to the harder things. In my opinion, adding a daily nutritional supplement routine to our lives is one of the easiest things we can do if we know the right things to take.

God made it simple in Genesis 1:29 when he described the herbs and fruits that should be our food. He made it simple again in Genesis 9:3 when he added fish to our diet. He also gave very specific directions in Deuteronomy 11 and Leviticus 14 about some of the things we should not eat. Did you know one in every three of God's laws in the Old Testament is related to health? Most of them are nutritional laws. Scientists today tell us that six of the ten major causes of disease are related to what we put in our mouths. It reminds us of Exodus 23:25–26, doesn't it? The blessing must first be on our food and water, and then God takes disease from the midst of us. Yet again, how can we get the blessing from our food if the nutritional value of that food is increasingly depleted? I believe the answer is to add those nutrients back into our diets through a regular, sound, and simple nutritional supplement program that we take with our regular meals.

Now, I know you can go to a health-food or vitamin store and wind up carrying off ten, fifteen, or even twenty-some bottles because you are really not sure what you need. Dealing with all of those bottles isn't easy either. But I believe God has a better plan.

How do we know what to take?

Here is how I simplify it. There are seven essential categories of sixty-three basic elements or groups you need to put into your body every day. I call them "The Seven Essential Complexes."

The Seven Essential Complexes

1. Vitamins and Basic Antioxidants
2. Minerals
3. Cell and Nervous System Complex
4. Fruit and Vegetable Extracts
5. Digestion and Absorption Enzymes
6. Super Antioxidants
7. Essential Fatty Acids

In the following sections I will discuss each of these complexes and a bit about what they address and how they work. For your reference, I have also included charts at the end of each section that list the nutrients in each category and their correct dosages. Please watch the dosages carefully—although with some things getting more is not an issue, with others getting too much can lead to adverse side effects.

You will also notice that some elements or compounds are repeated in these charts. This is because they have benefits that are specific in each area. This is why, for example, Bioperine® is listed under both "Digestion and Absorption Enzymes" and "Super Antioxidants," as it works wonderfully as a digestive enzyme but is also a potent antioxidant. For this reason as well, you will see that there are different dosages assigned for each function. Again, using Bioperine® as an example, you will see that I suggest taking 1 mg of it for digestion and another 5 mg for its antioxidant activity. So in total I would suggest you take 6 mg of Bioperine® to get its multiple benefits.

I have also included an "Index of Charts" after the contents page in the front of this book. This provides a quick reference to the elements suggested in this book as you discuss them with your doctor, health care professional, nutritionist, pharmacist, or whoever else helps you with your choice of dietary supplements. (Find someone who is knowledgable.)

VITAMINS AND BASIC ANTIOXIDANTS

Vitamins are typically the group we think of first when we talk about nutritional supplements, but this group also contains many antioxidants (vitamins A [in the form of beta carotene], C, and E, for example) that are essential for battling the free radicals in our bodies that are so common in our environment today. In general, antioxidants are produced naturally by our bodies but can also be found in numerous fruits and vegetables.

ANTIOXIDANTS: The main benefit of antioxidants is that they "clean up" the free radicals in our systems. Every cell in our body produces tens of thousands of free radicals daily. We also pick up free radicals in our environment through secondhand smoke and other pollutants. Left to themselves, these free radicals cause tremendous cell damage and can lead to a number of chronic ailments, including cancer, heart disease, cataracts, and stroke, among many others.

Free radicals are "renegade" oxygen molecules that have lost an electron and therefore wander about in our systems looking for an electron from somewhere else. When they find one, they throw whatever molecule they take the electron from into imbalance and change its structure. These "torn" or altered molecules then become problems for cells and often turn them cancerous. Within arteries they cause tears in the linings, which can trigger the blood to clot just as a cut in our skin triggers blood to clot to keep us from bleeding to death. This causes the vessel walls to thicken and can create major problems if these clots grow large enough to reduce blood flow, block it, or break off to lodge in other parts of the body, such as the brain or heart, and cause a heart attack or stroke. Antioxidants act by finding these free radicals before they do damage and "latch onto them" by giving them the electron they need and either escorting them out of our systems in this manner or releasing them as normal O_2 oxygen cells to be absorbed beneficially by our systems. By cleaning up these free radicals, antioxidants keep our systems more balanced, make useful oxygen more plentiful, keep the cardiovascular system strong, and reduce the chances of illness and the effects of aging. Free radicals are among the leading elements believed to cause aging.

Many of the antioxidants are called *flavonoids* or *bioflavonoids*. They are an important component in the new technology of nutritional supplements. They also tend to work in a somewhat different manner than other antioxidants. Vitamin C in particular has been proven effective in protecting test subjects from many types of cancer, especially internal cancers such as stomach, esophageal, and possibly colon cancer. In one study of nearly ten thousand men, those who got the most flavonoids from food sources were 20 percent less likely to develop any form of cancer and 46 percent less likely to develop lung cancer.

Flavonoids are found most prominently in various berries, broccoli, carrots, citrus fruits, peppers, tomatoes, apples, green tea, and various grape products, including red wine extract, grape-seed extract, and grape-skin extract. The natural chemicals contained in plants are referred to as *phytochemicals*.

There are some people groups in the world that have almost no cancer and almost no heart disease. When you study them, you find their diets are rich in the antioxidant beta carotene (a form of vitamin A). Vitamin E and C work together to lower heart disease risk. Studies across the board show that there is a higher incidence of heart disease among people with low levels of the antioxidants, such as E, C, beta carotene, and selenium. It appears these substances reduce the activity of platelets, the sticky elements that form clots inside the arteries, which can lead to heart attacks and strokes. Men given these types of antioxidants showed reductions of 20 to 50 percent in their measure of platelet activity.

Another recent study was done with physicians who were having some type of blockage in their arteries. They were put on beta carotene as a supplement, and they had 49 percent fewer heart attacks than those not on beta carotene. Beta carotene has also been shown to reduce the risk of lung, breast, and possibly colon cancer.

One of the leading causes of blindness in the world is cataracts. Fifty million people worldwide are blind because of cataracts. Surgery has been the only treatment for this condition until recently. In the U.S. alone, we perform over one-half million cataract operations per year, costing around $3.8 billion. One study shows that taking daily supplements of vitamins—particularly the antioxidants such as vitamin E and beta carotene—reduces the risk of cataracts by nearly 40 percent. We're simply increasing the dosage of something natural that God gave us to function as a type of drug and protector. Research from Ontario, Canada, indicates that vitamin E supplements can cut the incidence of cataracts by 50 percent.

God created a whole class of compounds that we are now able to incorporate in simple caplet, tablet, and capsule form. Take, for example, a class of antioxidants known as *carotenoids*. These include the familiar beta carotene we just discussed but also include compounds you may not be as familiar with, such as lutein, zeaxanthin, alpha-carotene, lycopene, and beta-cryptoxanthin. In addition to helping prevent cancer and hardening of the arteries, other studies have shown that the carotenoids lutein and zeaxanthin lower the risk of cataracts up to 22 percent. They block oxidative processes in the protein composition of the human lens.

Lutein and zeaxanthin are found in high concentrations in the eye tissue. In addition to helping protect us from cataracts, these two supplements also increase the macular pigment. They are beneficial in preventing, and perhaps even reversing, macular degeneration—which is becoming an increasingly common problem. We are now able not only to include these compounds in supplements, but we can include the extracts from foods that are typically high in carotenoid content, such as broccoli, spinach, blueberries, and cranberries.

You need to exercise caution when taking some of these compounds, however. I always encourage people to consult with a doctor who specializes in preventive medicine and gather solid information before starting to take anything on a regular basis. Vitamin C, for example, can be a problem if you've had kidney stones. One study shows that beta carotene can be harmful to smokers. It actually makes them more susceptible to cancer rather than less.

B-VITAMINS AND BIOTIN: As we get older, it is quite common for our absorption of many of the B-vitamins to decrease. These are primarily folate (folic acid), B_6, and B_{12}. Studies have documented that low levels of these vitamins will adversely affect your memory. Folic acid is particularly important because it decreases homocysteine, an amino acid that breaks down serotonin, which is a key neurotransmitter that helps cells talk to each other. Low serotonin levels have been directly related to such things as depression, insomnia, migraine headaches, and other problems (see the following chapters for more information on the importance of serotonin to the function of the brain and nervous system). B_6 is a nerve supplement that has been used to combat the nerve damage in the wrists caused by carpal tunnel syndrome and has been used to keep nerves strong in the brain and throughout the rest of the body. B_{12} has been called the "senility vitamin" because it has such a potent effect on counteracting the effects of aging on nerve cells.

B-vitamins also have a role to play in healthy vision—B_2 and B_3 protect glutathione, an important antioxidant. B-vitamins (especially B_6) also lower homocysteine, which has become a major factor correlated with the risk of heart disease. They also help counter the tendency of arteries to constrict after meals, which can bring on chronic heart disease events. The B-vitamins are needed for energy metabolism, while B_6 is essential for amino acid metabolism, neurotransmitter (brain chemicals) synthesis, glycogen utilization, and immune function; and B_{12} is crucial for cell formation and cell division.

Biotin is a B-vitamin that plays a role in the formation of fatty acids and the release of energy from carbohydrates as well as being important for healthy skin, hair, and nails.

VITAMIN D: Vitamin D has long been touted as crucial to strong bones and teeth because it helps in the absorption and use of calcium. This, of course, makes it crucial to those concerned with osteoporosis or other diseases affecting their bones and becomes more important as we grow older. Vitamin D has also been shown to strengthen the immune system, slow the joint damage caused by arthritis, ease back pain, protect against multiple sclerosis, relieve symptoms of psoriasis, and may prevent some types of cancer.

Strangely enough, our bodies produce much of the vitamin D we need from sunlight—roughly fifteen minutes of sunlight a few days a week will give us all we need. Despite this, as many as 57 percent of young adults in America are likely to be somewhat deficient in this vitamin. For this reason I have included it in our list, but you should not exceed the recommended dosage, as it can have some adverse side effects if taken in too high a quantity.[1]

VITAMIN E: We've already discussed vitamin E as an antioxidant, but we also need to discuss it individually to further understand its benefits. What we refer to as vitamin E is actually a tocopherol. There are four different forms of tocopherol and four forms of tocotrienols (which could more correctly be called vitamin E's "cousins"). Other than d-alpha tocopherol, which is natural vitamin E, God created seven other forms that all work together. This is exactly why certain recent studies have shown vitamin E is not very effective in treating or preventing heart disease; they are testing just one of these eight compounds, not all eight working together. The truth is that vitamin E is effective in treating heart disease, but only if several of its forms are taken together. Natural vitamin E has to work in balance with its other forms and other vitamins to maximize effectiveness.

Vitamin E also shows potential as a major cholesterol killer. In other words, vitamin E prevents the chemical change that happens when cholesterol interacts with free radicals and therefore protects the arteries from the fat deposits that can clog your veins and arteries. If we simply look at these substances as vitamins, we could perhaps get enough in our food. But in the higher dosages that we're talking about, we are actually presenting them as a prescription to protect us from the onslaught of disease.

Another research study out of Israel reported that high doses of vitamin E elevated the good, or protective, HDL cholesterol level, which tends to pull cholesterol from the arteries and take it to the liver, where it is broken down. Vitamin E has also been cited in work done at the National Cancer Institute as a neutralizer of nitrates. Nitrates are found in foods such as bacon and other processed meat products and have been indicated in causing cancer.

An English study shows that the higher the vitamin E level in the human body, the less the incidence of breast cancer. At Tufts University Medical School, vitamin E bolstered or increased the immune system. Another group at Albany Medical College, a well-respected medical institution, showed vitamin E slowing the progression of Parkinson's disease. Countless other studies are showing vitamin E has benefits for numerous other body systems as well. This wide range of benefits has caused some to call vitamin E "the miracle vitamin."[2]

The following chart lists the specific vitamins and antioxidants (and their dosages) that I suggest taking on a regular basis:

Vitamin & Basic Antioxidant Complex	Strength
1. Natural mixed carotenoids (Caromix™-alpha-carotene, lycopene, lutein)	2,000 mcg
2. Vitamin A (as beta carotene, dunaliella salina, zeaxanthin, retinyl palmitate)	25,000 IU
3. Vitamin B_1 (as thiamine mononitrate)	50 mg
4. Vitamin B_2 (as riboflavin, riboflavin-5-phosphate)	50 mg
5. Vitamin B_3 (niacin: as inositol hexaniacinate, niacinamide)	100 mg
6. Vitamin B_5 (pantothenic acid: as d-calcium pantothenate)	50 mg
7. Vitamin B_6 (as pyridoxine HCI, pyridoxal-5-phosphate)	75 mg
8. Vitamin B_{12} (as cyanocobalamin, dibencozide)	100 mcg
9. Biotin	300 mcg
10. Folate (as folic acid)	600 mcg
11. Vitamin C (as ascorbic acid, calcium ascorbate, acerola cherry)	2,040 mg
12. Vitamin D_3 (as cholecalciferol)	400 IU

| 13. Vitamin E (as natural d-alpha tocopheryl succinate, natural mixed tocopherols) | 800 IU |

MINERALS

Although we are not always as concerned with getting the minerals we need as much as we are of getting the right vitamins, minerals may well be more important than vitamins to our various systems and affect more of the twenty-two major health concerns than vitamins do. Minerals are also becoming more and more depleted in the foods we eat; getting the right minerals through supplements is definitely crucial to maintaining a strong and healthy body.

CALCIUM: Calcium helps keep teeth, bones, and joints strong and healthy, in addition to feeding our muscles and nerves. It is crucial for preventing osteoporosis and gout, a very acutely painful form of arthritis that primarily affects the joints in the feet. It can also help protect us from high blood pressure and prevent heart irregularities. Calcium has also been shown to protect the colon from cancer and have a calming effect, especially on children struggling with attention-deficit hyperactivity disorder (ADHD). I recommend taking it in a citrate and gluconate form simply because of their varying absorption rates and varying amounts. Also avoid taking it solely in the form of carbonate because it can overly dilute stomach acid.

CHROMIUM: Chromium, which is a trace mineral found prominently in baker's yeast and several other products, has been shown to have multiple effects and benefits on diabetes. Chromium tends to decrease blood sugar levels and decrease the severity of diabetes. It is also crucial to helping the body use insulin correctly. More than twenty-five well-controlled clinical trials have demonstrated that chromium can regulate healthy glucose levels in the body. Sadly enough, up to 25 percent of the American population is deficient in chromium, which may well be a major contributor to the increase in diabetes we have seen in this country. Vanadium and alpha lipoic acid (ALA) work together with chromium to help prevent diabetes by stabilizing abnormal blood sugar levels.

Chromium also has an effect on lowering total cholesterol and LDL cholesterol (which we call the bad cholesterol) levels because it is important for activating enzymes in the body for fat metabolism. Chromium helps prevent the formation of new fatty cells from carbohydrates, helps optimize the metabolism or breakdown of glucose, helps balance sugar levels between meals, and helps increase and promote lean body mass and healthy cholesterol levels. It also seems to decrease the effects of aging.

TAKE ELEMENTS IN COMBINATION FOR BEST RESULTS: As with many of the substances discussed in this chapter, it is best to take chromium in combination with other elements. One of the reasons I believe God put so many different nutrients into the same foods is that we are designed to use them in concert with one another. Chromium, for instance, functions best when combined with vitamin E and a good multivitamin with extra doses of C, beta carotene, and selenium. There was a report released recently from the University of Alabama and presented at the American Chemical Society that indicated that chromium could cause potential DNA damage. The report indicated that a certain type of hydroxyl radical was formed in the body. The basic problem with studies of this type is that they use one supplement in high dosages without combining the supplement with other various antioxidants.

COPPER: Copper is a mineral essential to connective and joint tissues, immune function, and nerve cells. It is the third most abundant trace mineral in the body. Research has shown that it also has benefits for staving off heart rhythm disorders (arrhythmia) and high blood pressure, reducing arthritis symptoms, and that it may minimize loss in mineral bone density over time, a development that can lead to osteoporosis. One of the cautions with copper that we will discuss later in this section is that it should always be kept in proper balance with your zinc intake.

IODINE: The main function of iodine is to keep the thyroid gland healthy so that it is able to manufacture thyroxine, a hormone that helps to regulate metabolism, to control the physical and mental growth of children, and to break down fats and proteins. Pregnant women need to watch their iodine levels because insufficient iodine can cause cretinism in a fetus. Iodine is also, at least indirectly, responsible for the proper function of some of the most elementary biological functions of the body.

MAGNESIUM: Magnesium has been shown helpful in treating high blood pressure, migraine headaches, and coronary artery disease. Magnesium is a natural calcium channel blocker, which slows down the uptake of calcium in the small, smooth-muscle lining of arteries and thus relaxes them. It works alongside proper calcium and potassium intake to lower blood pressure readings. This has the effect of dilating the vessels (arteries), thus reducing the risk of their hardening. This effect alone is tremendously helpful because so many diseases are related to hardening of the arteries. Magnesium also improves the absorption of insulin and thus has tremendous benefits for those struggling with diabetes.

A study of eighty-one people with a history of migraine headaches who were treated with magnesium showed a 42 percent drop in the incidence of these headaches in just three months. Migraine headaches are caused by changes in blood vessels. Magnesium also inhibits the formation of calcium oxalate, which is one of the chemical combinations that contributes to the formation of kidney stones. Magnesium has also been shown to decrease the symptoms of PMS as well as decrease the fluid retention that is associated with PMS. It has also been shown helpful for those suffering from restless leg syndrome.

POTASSIUM: In addition to helping magnesium regulate blood pressure, potassium is an electrolyte that is important for fluid balance and nerve cell impulse conduction. The body fluids absorb it and take it into the cells, where it is used to help release energy. It helps transmit impulses that signal muscle movements and heart contractions. This is why too much potassium can have the side effect of irregular heartbeats and muscle weakness.

SELENIUM: Selenium is a mineral that acts as an antioxidant. It has shown good results in treating heart disease and cancer because of its antioxidant activity. This is one to be careful with, however, as selenium can be toxic if received in too high a dosage. It can actually cause cancer if you exceed the recommended amount on a regular basis over time.

SILICA: This mineral is important in the development and maintenance of bones, nails, teeth, connective tissues, hair, and skin. Horsetail, a flowerless plant of which silica is a key part, has also been shown to have a positive effect in treating Crohn's disease.

ZINC: Many people, particularly as they get older, do not get enough zinc in their diet.

Zinc is strongly protective of immune system function, but unless you get about a 10:2 to 10:1 ratio of zinc to copper you're going to be in trouble. If you get too much zinc and not enough copper you're out of balance. Excess zinc can also be a potential contributing factor to the development of Alzheimer's disease. So don't go out and take large quantities of zinc. Fifteen milligrams will give your immune system the maximum benefit and will not have adverse side effects.

TRACE MINERALS: There are several minerals of which our bodies need only a small amount, or trace. These are called trace minerals. The most significant of these are magnesium, selenium, and zinc, which we have already discussed in some detail. The others that I believe are important to our daily nutrition are boron, manganese, molybdenum, and vanadium. Boron has been shown to strengthen bones and joints. Manganese also helps with connective or joint tissue and acts as an antioxidant in the circulatory system to fight free radicals. Molybdenum is important to many key metabolic pathways. We also need vanadium, which counteracts the symptoms of diabetes because it supports insulin function and glucose regulation.

There are also some cautions to consider with these trace elements. Boron can raise the risk of breast or prostate cancer because of its effects on hormone levels. Manganese can have a toxic effect for any who suffer from liver or gallbladder disease. Molybdenum can worsen gout symptoms.[3]

Most trace minerals don't have negative side effects, even when taken in large doses. Others, however, do. Too much manganese can result in severe psychiatric symptoms, violent rages, poor coordination, and stiff muscles. More than 500 mg a day of boron can cause nausea, vomiting, diarrhea, and fatigue. Dosages of vanadium higher than 10 mg a day can lead to cramping, diarrhea, and a green tongue.[4]

The following chart lists all of the minerals I recommend taking on a daily basis along with the dosage I would prescribe for each:

Minerals Complex	Strength
1. Boron (as boron glycinate, boron aspartate, boron citrate)	2,000 mcg
2. Calcium (as calcium carbonate, calcium citrate, calcium ascorbate, calcium gluconate)	1,000 mg
3. Chromium (as chromium nicotinate, Chromium Picolinate™)	300 mcg
4. Copper (as copper citrate)	2 mg
5. Iodine (as potassium iodide)	150 mcg
6. Magnesium (as magnesium oxide, magnesium citrate, magnesium alpha-ketoglutarate)	400 mg
7. Manganese (as manganese citrate)	7.5 mg
8. Molybdenum (as molybdenum citrate)	75 mcg
9. Potassium (as potassium citrate)	99 mg
10. Selenium (as I-selenomethionine)	200 mcg
11. Silica	7.5 mg
12. Trace Minerals (as marine mineral complex-Hydromins®)	50 mg
13. Vanadium (as vanadyl sulfate)	300 mcg
14. Zinc (as zinc citrate)	15 mg

CELL AND NERVOUS SYSTEM COMPLEX

The nervous system is so highly specialized that it needs its own unique supplements in light of the fact that memory and brain function problems are on the rise, especially as the baby-boomer generation gets older. We need such things as choline and phosphatidylserine to protect against age-related memory loss (ARML), dementia, and Alzheimer's disease. Many elements that help our brains have the double blessing of also being beneficial to the cardiovascular system.

Phosphatidylserine is the concentrated component of lecithin. It is rich in choline, which produces the extremely important chemical *acetylcholine,* essential for memory function. Phosphatidylserine, choline, and inositol are important components guarding our brain and nervous system function that I believe should be in our daily supplement program. Phosphatidylserine can improve concentration and our ability to recall names and faces. It may also improve brain function in early Alzheimer's disease.

Choline actually acts like a B-vitamin that helps transport fats and nutrients into and out of cells, and forms cell membranes. It produces the extremely important chemical *acetylcholine*, which is so essential for memory function; it is often called the "memory molecule." Because of this function it is also critical to fetal and infant development and is in all FDA-approved infant formulas. Choline also aids in fat metabolism.

The following chart lists the dosages I recommend of these key elements for our brain and nervous system's proper function:

Cell and Nervous System Complex	Strength
1. Choline (as dihydrogen citrate)	250 mg
2. Inositol (as inositol crystalline)	50 mg
3. Phosphatidylserine	100 mcg

FRUIT AND VEGETABLE EXTRACTS

The elements in this category show some of the great strides modern science has made in the area of nutrition. While the nutritional value of our food is diminishing, technology has enabled us to take the concentrated extracts of fruits and vegetables and put them into supplement form. While taking these supplements will not completely replace the fruits and vegetables we need to have in our diets, they do take us a long way toward getting the recommended servings of fruits and vegetables we should be getting every day. In other words, we go straight back to Genesis 1:29—God has given us everything we need in the plants and fruits of the earth.

Taken twice daily, fruit and vegetable extracts have been shown to increase immune system cells and their activity, specifically the T cells and NK (natural killer) cells that are essential in fighting bacteria, infections, viruses, and cancer-causing agents. Did you know that one medical theory states that we develop cancer cells in our bodies almost every day? This theory reasons that cells very likely go haywire on a regular basis because of the myriad of cell divisions taking place every day. It is in these "haywired" cells that cancer can get started—*except* that our strong immune systems, which God placed within us as a first-line defense mechanism to deal with these abnormal cells, eliminates them almost as fast as they are formed. This is part of the reason that if we have a weakened immune system, we are more susceptible to cancer spreading to the point that it can endanger our lives. Other studies show that DNA damage (which is one of the causes of cancer) in the lymphocytes, or white blood cells, decreases by 60 percent after taking fruit and vegetable extracts over a period of time.

Because the immune system also tends to weaken as we get older, taking fruit and vegetable extracts can be even more critical. Consuming these extracts as part of a daily basic nutrient supplement gives the added bonus of maintaining a consistent level of these protective compounds in our bloodstream. You can't do this simply by eating them at every meal because your level will go up and down depending on the nutrients in the foods you are eating each time. It is possible to take these extracts from over twenty-five different fruits and vegetables. While it can be difficult to consume the five to nine portions of fruits and vegetables recommended daily, taking extracts of these can be done quite easily with each meal.

According to the head of clinical nutrition research at Memorial Sloan/Kettering Cancer Center and Weill Medical College of Cornell, the day is here when we can prescribe these natural chemical compounds to prevent or even cure cancer. A massive international analysis in 1997 found more than two hundred studies linking various vegetables and fruits to cancer prevention. Again, the foods that turn up frequently in this category include tomatoes, tea (particularly green tea), and various vitamins and minerals such as vitamin E and selenium.

The phytochemicals found in various berries also protect us from atherosclerosis (hardening or clogging of the arteries), heart disease, and stroke by reducing the oxidation of the LDL, or bad cholesterol. Topping the list in this category are red raspberries, cherries, blueberries, and strawberries. Extracts of all of these are available in a simple tablet form and can be taken on a daily basis for health protection.

OLIVE LEAF EXTRACT: Another natural protection for body cells is found in the extract of the olive leaf. The olive tree, found in Mediterranean countries, secretes compounds that protect it from various bacteria, fungi, parasites, and insects.

This leaf extract has been used for decades. Its active ingredient, *oleuropein,* provides natural protection for the cells and actually has an antibiotic or antibacterial effect. We are now able to place this extract in a daily supplement tablet for the additional protection that our bodies need in these challenging days.

The following chart lists the fruit, vegetable, and plant extracts I recommend taking together and their dosages:

Fruit & Vegetable Extracts Complex	Strength
1. Fruits and Greens Powder (apricot, bing cherry, cranberry, grapefruit, golden delicious apple, Hawaiian pineapple, lemon, lime, orange, peach, red raspberry, red wine grape, rubini berry, strawberry, wild blueberry, broccoli, Brussels sprout, cabbage, carrot, celery stalk, Jersey tomato, kale, rosemary, spinach)	300 mg
2. Olive Leaf Extract (*Olea europaea*)	20 mg

DIGESTION AND ABSORPTION ENZYMES

The salivary glands, the stomach, the walls of the small intestine, and the pancreas all produce enzymes that break down the food we eat into nutrients our bodies can absorb. We also get enzymes that aid in the digestion and absorption of food from the fruits and vegetables we eat. Both of these groups are crucial to the proper digestion of the foods we consume.

As we grow older, our digestive system, especially the pancreas, begins producing fewer and fewer enzymes. Certain diseases such as diabetes and coronary heart disease also affect the functions and production of the enzymes our bodies produce. God, however, gave us enzymes within the plant kingdom that do the same thing as our natural pancreatic enzymes.

Any basic nutrient support program should also include specific compounds for the digestion and absorption of the vitamins, minerals, extracts, and other elements included in the tablets and capsules. By including various digestive enzymes such as amylase, protease, lipase, lactase, and cellulase within the supplement, we are able to absorb the ingredients even better and improve our overall digestion as well.

BIOPERINE®: A simple pepper extract, bioperine, can help you absorb a wide range of nutrients. Another of its main functions is that it helps thermogenesis, which is the metabolic process that generates energy in the cells. This contributes to weight loss as well as providing more energy for all the systems of the body. This is a great addition to any nutritional supplement as it also helps us digest and absorb all of the other vitamins, minerals, extracts, and nutrients in supplement tablets or capsules, making them much more effective and beneficial.

BROMELAIN: Protein is one of the hardest nutrients to break down and absorb. Protein is very essential for muscle building and various body functions, but it's much more difficult to break down than fats or carbohydrates. So the pancreas produces enzymes such as trypsin and chymotrypsin to break down proteins. As we get older, though, the pancreas secretes fewer and fewer of these enzymes. The best alternative to replacing this comes from the plant kingdom, where there are many natural enzymes. Bromelain is one of these and is very beneficial because it breaks down protein just as effectively as your own pancreatic enzymes.

Bromelain is an enzyme found in the stem of the pineapple plant. In addition to helping with the proper functioning of the digestive tract, bromelain is also an anti-inflammatory substance. It inhibits a class of chemicals in the body known as *kinins* and *fibrin*, which cause inflammation in the body. There have been several studies showing a decrease in sport injuries because of bromelain. For example, one study done with boxers showed a decrease of bruising in the body. Several scientists have discovered a positive effect of bromelain on shingles. Shingles is caused by the old virus that causes chicken pox. It gets inside the nerves and remains inactive for years until we experience periods of stress later in life, during which it is triggered. This is a very, very painful form of nerve irritation. Bromelain, functioning again as an anti-inflammatory, can decrease the inflammation that occurs in these nerve endings. Because bromelain functions as an anti-inflammatory, it also has some benefits in treating gout, joint problems, and arthritis.

There are studies from around the world where people didn't have access to Acyclovir—which is a common antiviral prescription drug—or some of the other prescription medicines to reduce inflammation. When bromelain was compared with Acyclovir, bromelain worked just about as well as the prescription drug. So this is another reason that I personally take this every day and recommend our patients do the same, as it has multiple benefits.

There are four or five placebo control studies that were done observing subjects who had been diagnosed with chronic sinusitis. These compared a group who were on bromelain with groups who underwent traditional medical treatments for sinusitis. Those in the bromelain group actually came out just as well as those treated with antibiotics and various other things but had fewer side effects.

CINNAMON: Cinnamon has been used for centuries for digestive purposes, especially in the Orient. It comes from the bark of a tree. It not only enhances digestion but also increases the activity of insulin. Cinnamon contains catechins, which fight cancer and heart disease as well as help relieve nausea. The oil from cinnamon bark also breaks down the fats in foods and stimulates movement in the gastrointestinal tract. It also reduces gas in the system to a mild extent and can help with flatulence and the feelings of bloatedness connected with excess gas in the digestive system. It has also been reported to boost appetite and increase salivary function.

FENNEL SEED: Fennel has long been used as a spice for things from breads to teas and has been associated with helping in digestion and relieving upset stomachs, gas, and coughs. It is also being investigated as a natural source from which to derive estrogen. I recommend including it in your daily supplement plan primarily for its general support and benefit to the digestive system.

GLUCONO-DELTA-LACTONE: This enzyme promotes the healthy growth of microflora bacteria in your intestines. It's called a prebiotic because it supplies food to these good bacteria. It can be found in honey, fruit juices, wine, and many fermented products. It is a natural acid that contributes to the tangy flavor of various foods. Since it lowers the pH level, it is also used as a natural preservative.

PAPAIN: Papain comes from the papaya plant and has similar benefits as bromelain in helping to break down proteins. Both of these enzymes are known as proteolytic enzymes, which simply means they help digest the proteins in food. Because of this effect on proteins, they are both traditionally used as a meat tenderizer. Papain has been used to treat ulcers, dissolve membranes in diphtheria, and to reduce swelling, fever, or adhesions after surgery.

Perhaps the strongest evidence for benefits of proteolytic enzyme supplements comes from numerous European studies that have shown the benefits of various enzymes working together to accelerate the recovery from athletic injuries as well as facilitate tissue repair in patients following surgery. In one study of soccer players suffering from ankle injuries, proteolytic enzyme supplements shortened the time it took to heal and got them back on the field about 50 percent faster than athletes assigned to receive a placebo tablet. A handful of other small trials in athletes have shown these enzymes can help reduce inflammation, speed the healing of bruises and other tissue injuries (including fractures), and reduce the overall recovery time from such injuries. In patients recovering from facial and various reconstructive surgeries, treatment with proteolytic enzymes was shown to significantly reduce swelling, bruising, and stiffness.[5]

PEPPERMINT LEAF EXTRACT: Another important digestive tract ingredient is peppermint extract. It helps relax the intestinal tract and enhances the digestive processes.

While peppermint extract is helpful as a daily supplement, I have also suggested enteric-coated peppermint oil capsules as an herbal treatment for irritable bowel syndrome or spastic colon. Research has indicated that the oil found in the peppermint plant can relax smooth muscle in the colon. The prescription muscle relaxants (known as antispas-modics) cause numerous side effects, but the peppermint oil found in the plant kingdom has no serious side effects. Research done in Britain and recorded in the medical journal *Lancet* showed that spasms in the colon were reduced by nearly 50 percent after the oil was introduced into the colon. The capsules are available in a standardized coated form that contains 0.2 ml of peppermint oil. One to two capsules daily between meals would be the recommended treatment if you were suffering from irritability or spasms in the colon.

GLUCOMANNAN PROPOL™: We now also have the ability to put a soluble fiber, Pro-pol™—which is a glucomannan—into supple-ments to help lower cholesterol. It comes from the root of a plant in Japan called the konjac plant. When it is taken, it expands in the stomach and absorbs cholesterol, bile acids, and heavy metals, thus preventing them from being absorbed in the intestines and helping them to be eliminated from the body. As a result, the serum cholesterol and serum triglyceride levels may be reduced. It also has the added benefit of satisfying your appetite because your stomach feels full.

The following chart shows the compounds I recommend and the daily recommended dosages of each for your daily supplement program:

Digestion & Absorption Complex	Strength
1. Bioperine® (Black Pepper Extract)	1 mg
2. Bromelain	50 mg
3. Ceylon Cinnamon Bark Powder (*Cinnammomum zeylanicum*)	80 mg
4. Fennel Seed Powder (*Foeniculum vulgare*)	80 mg
5. Glucono-Delta-Lactone	300 mg
6. Multi-Enzyme Complex (amylase, protease, lipase, cellulase, lactase, alpha galactosidase)	50 mg
7. Papain	25 mg
8. Peppermint Leaf Powder (*Mentha piperita*)	80 mg
9. Glucomannan Propol™ (Amorphophallus konjac root)	150 mg

SUPER ANTIOXIDANTS

There is a whole new class of antioxidants that are now called the super antioxidants. The basic four antioxidants are vitamin C, vitamin E, beta carotene, and selenium. Now we have found that things like alpha lipoic acid (ALA), CoQ10, lycopene, and quercetin also have extremely potent antioxidant qualities but with other benefits as well.

ALPHA LIPOIC ACID (ALA): Alpha lipoic acid is a potent antioxidant because it produces energy in the muscles and helps direct calories into energy production. ALA is concentrated in structures in our cells called the mitochondria, which actually produce the energy inside body cells, especially the muscle cells. What we want to do is concentrate as much ALA as possible in these muscle cells. This is particularly important with diabetics because they can't get enough glucose into their muscle cells and into the peripheral tissue. This causes them to run out of energy. ALA works very well to counteract that.

ALA also regenerates vitamins E and C. That is one reason you want to take vitamins C and E in combination with a balanced preparation that includes ALA. There appears to be more and more publicity about how individual vitamins are not very effective, and this confuses many people. There is now increasing evidence that just taking vitamin E or vitamin C alone may be more harmful than taking nothing at all. A couple of the main reasons for these findings are that they are testing the vitamins in isolation or they are testing just one form of the vitamin that is not particularly beneficial. God did not place vitamin E, such as d-alpha tocopherol, which is the chemical name of its natural form, by itself in nature. He combined it with numerous other compounds. When vitamin E gets depleted, certain other compounds regenerate it, and that's why the balance has to take place with supplements. God did not design these elements to be taken alone. He put them in combinations in the food we eat because they are all supposed to work together and support each other to keep sickness and disease away from us. ALA is one of the substances that support other nutrients.

ALA also helps sustain normal blood sugar levels and supports proper nervous system function as well as proper liver function. Although our body makes this nutrient, it is often not produced in the amount we need, and getting the right amount of it through foods alone has proven difficult. This is why I suggest taking it in concentrated form as part of your daily supplement program.

BILBERRY POWDER: Bilberry, a close relative of the American blueberry, grows in northern Europe, Canada, and parts of the United States. The ripe berries have wonderful benefits, but the leaves also contain helpful compounds. Bilberries are high in a bioflavonoid complex known as *anthocyanosides* and are potent antioxidants that speed the regeneration of *rhodopsin*, the purple pigment that is used by the rods in the eye for night vision. Long made into jam in Europe and Asia, bilberries were actually pressed into service during World War II when British fighter pilots reported improved night vision four to six weeks after eating bilberry jam.

In parts of Europe, bilberry extract is widely prescribed for the prevention and treatment of eye disorders of all types, including macular degeneration, glaucoma, poor night vision, diabetic retinopathy, blood-vessel thickening due to diabetes, and cataracts. Bilberry is also thought to be useful for treating varicose veins and excessive bruising, accelerating wound healing, alleviating hemorrhoids, and preventing heart disease. It even prevents cholesterol from oxidizing. Bilberry also has no known side effects.

BROCCOLI AND CABBAGE POWDERS: Broccoli is one of the most nutritious foods that you can eat. It has traditionally been a central figure in the Mediterranean diet. Not only does it have a rich supply of vitamins and minerals such as vitamin C, folic acid, and potassium, but it also contains sulforaphane, various other sulphur compounds, indole-3-carbinols, and gultaphon, which have all been shown to significantly reduce the risk of various forms of cancer. It is also a source of lutein, beta carotene, carotenoids, and flavonoids as well as a multitude of other beneficial elements that science has yet to completely identify.

Cabbage is an excellent source of vitamin C and contains significant amounts of the nitrogen compounds known as indoles, which appear to lower the risk of various forms of cancer. Cabbage contains sulforaphane, as does broccoli. Cabbage also has a good amount of both soluble and insoluble fiber.

While each of these vegetables should be a part of our normal weekly menus, taking them in concentrated extract form every day will keep a consistent level of their beneficial compounds in our systems and give us a great head start on the recommended five to nine servings of fruits and vegetables we should eat every day.

CITRUS BIOFLAVONOID COMPLEX AND RUTIN: Citrus fruits contain many different types of flavonoids. Dr. Fotsis at the University of Ioannina in Greece found that certain citric flavonoids would actually cut off the blood supply to tumors, helping to eliminate them naturally. Research in Japan has identified two flavonoids (diosmin and hesperidin), which are especially effective against cancer in the oral cavity. With the addition of the benefits of vitamin C normally associated with citrus fruits, these extracts make tremendous sense as a part of our normal supplement program.

The citrus flavonoid *rutin* is another powerful antioxidant and is important for our eyes. It reportedly increases the effectiveness of conventional medication in glaucoma patients. Citrus bioflavonoids not containing pure rutin, pure hesperidin, or both are often less potent.

COENZYME Q10 (UBIQUINONE): Another important compound is *ubiquinone*, which is also known as Coenzyme Q10 (commonly abbreviated "CoQ10"). This was originally found to be beneficial in congestive heart failure and in strengthening the heart muscle.

Research has now indicated that CoQ10 may also be helpful in cancer treatment and prevention. CoQ10 has been shown to decrease PSA levels in patients with prostate cancer. Benefits have been reported in patients with stomach cancer and breast cancer. It also seems to enhance our immune system function. Because of all of these benefits, CoQ10 cannot be neglected as an essential component of any daily nutritional supplement.

GLUTATHIONE AND N-ACETYL-L-CYSTEINE: Glutathione is a small protein composed of three amino acids: cysteine, glutamic acid, and glycine. It binds to fat-soluble toxins, such as heavy metals, solvents, and pesticides, and transforms them into a water-soluble form that can be excreted through the urine. It also neutralizes free radicals and peroxide molecules and recharges oxidized vitamin C so that it can be absorbed into the body. This makes it a very effective detoxifier for our bodies. It is also essential to many metabolic processes. It is a great benefit to our immune systems, especially the lymphocyte immune cells. Research is also currently exploring how glutathione can be used to help treat diseases such as cancer, heart disease, memory loss, osteoarthritis, Parkinson's disease, cornea disorders, kidney dysfunction, eczema, liver disorders, poisoning by heavy metals, and immunodepression that occurs in diseases such as AIDS.[6]

The lenses of our eyes also depend on the antioxidant coenzyme glutathione for maintenance of their protein structure. Glutathione is abundant in the healthy lens and performs several crucial functions. It protects the sulfur-containing proteins from oxidizing, aids in the constant exchange of sodium, potassium, and calcium moving in and out of the lens cells, and slows the breakdown of DNA, assisting in flexibility maintenance. When the exchange of these vital minerals is interrupted and/or the sulfur-containing proteins oxidize, the eye's lens becomes inflexible and cloudy. The lens of the eye is a living component that under ideal circumstances retains its ability to change shape while still remaining transparent.

N-acetyl-L-cysteine is an amino acid that is actually a precursor to glutathione and contributes to glutathione production and retention. It makes the body's use of glutathione much more effective and is an important antioxidant and detoxifier in the body.

GRAPE-SEED AND GRAPE-SKIN EXTRACTS: We are hearing a lot these days about the benefits of non-alcoholic red wine and grape juice. God has given us the technology to now place the extracts from both grape seeds and grape skin into our daily supplements.

Grape-seed extract contains a special class of water-soluble flavonoids known as *proanthocyanidins,* which can specifically help fight the free radicals that cause aging. We still recommend small amounts (6 ounces) of either grape juice or alcohol-free red wine, but we can now be certain of maintaining constant blood levels of the various protective compounds found in the grapes by taking them in supplement form.

GREEN TEA EXTRACT: Another extremely interesting development is the research being done on green tea. *Nature* magazine recently reported research on an enzyme known as *urokinase,* which is used by cancer cells to help the cancer cell invade our normal body cells and spread. Green tea contains unique flavonoids known as catechins. The catechins in green tea actually prevent this enzyme from working and thus prevent the spread of cancer cells.

It might be difficult to drink 3–4 glasses of green tea daily, but God has now given us the wisdom and technology to incorporate green tea extracts into our daily nutrient supplement. We are now recommending green tea extract be part of everyone's daily intake because of the incredible research showing the benefits of green tea and catechins.

LYCOPENE AND TOMATO POWDER: Lycopene is the pigment in tomatoes that gives them their color. It is part of the carotenoid family, which is the name given to some of the pigments that give the red, yellow, or orange color to various fruits and vegetables. They have come to the attention of the medical community in recent years because studies have shown them to reduce the risk of heart disease, cancer, cataracts, macular degeneration, and strengthen the immune system in general. As a powerful antioxidant, lycopene is also believed to have positive effects on several problems presented by aging. For men, lycopene also helps in maintaining proper prostate gland function.

Studies seem to strongly suggest that lycopene may well be the most effective dietary carotenoid for turning free radicals back into useful oxygen molecules. So by including lycopene extract and tomato powder in a basic daily nutritional program we can address a number of ills. This is also a good reason to make sure you are eating tomato paste and sauces regularly in your diet, as they seem to be even better sources of lycopene than fresh tomatoes.

PARA-AMINOBENZOIC ACID (PABA): This nutrient, commonly referred to as PABA, is a member of the B-vitamin family and part of folic acid. It is synthesized naturally in the intestines by good bacteria there but can also be obtained through some grains and animal products. It plays a role in breaking down and using proteins, in forming red blood cells, supports proper cell growth and development, and is important for healthy hair and skin. It is probably most widely recognized as an ingredient in sunscreen products, where it has been shown to protect the skin by blocking damaging ultraviolet rays. However, because its use has also caused some irritation and allergic reactions in certain individuals, its popularity has somewhat diminished. People taking sulfa antibiotics should be careful when using PABA as it can interfere with the absorption of these medications.

QUERCETIN: Scientists were baffled for years about why apples and onions decreased allergy and hay fever symptoms. As it turns out, it is because apples and onions—and also green tea and grapes, among other elements—have a compound in them called *quercetin*.

Quercetin is a bioflavonoid compound that helps balance the immune system to fight such things as allergies, hay fever, and asthma. It also seems to help with elevated blood pressure. Being a cousin of green tea, it increases the body's metabolism and can have an effect on decreasing body weight. It is actually a natural antihistamine. One benefit of quercetin is that it doesn't make you drowsy, as do most pharmaceutical antihistamines.

The incidence of allergies is skyrocketing in this country, as is the incidence of asthma. Many scientists feel that allergies are increasing dramatically because we face more pollutants, dust mites, and other things today that throw the immune system out of balance. For example, your body should not recognize a small piece of pollen as being a foreign invader that is going to harm you, yet because of the intensity of foreign things we are breathing today, the immune system overreacts to even harmless things, which is the root cause of allergies. Quercetin will stop that reaction, and because of that most scientists now feel this flavonoid should actually be included in a daily balanced supplement.

VITAMIN E AND TOCOTRIENOLS: Another nutrient that has some amazing benefits to the cardiovascular as well as other body systems is vitamin E and its cousins, the tocotrienols. We used to simply recommend that people take vitamin E, but we now have more enlightenment on the whole family of vitamin-E compounds.

Natural d-alpha tocopherol is the form of vitamin E we should take daily. This form counters the effects of COX-2 and prosta-glandin E2, which promote inflammation. The natural d-alpha form should not be taken alone, however, but should be combined with naturally mixed tocopherols as well as the less familiar compounds known as tocotrienols. In nature, the tocopherols and tocotrienols always occur together, and they work best when taken together in a supplement. Together these compounds are proving to be extremely important in maintaining health. The key tocotrienols include alpha, beta, gamma, and delta tocotrienols.

The structures of the tocotrienols differ from the structure of the basic vitamin E molecule, giving them other specific functions of their own. For one, they tend to inhibit an enzyme known as HMG-CoA reductase. By inhibiting this enzyme, the body's production of cholesterol is decreased and thus total cholesterol levels are lowered. They also maintain proper health in the breast tissue and help maintain cell membranes of heart and skeletal muscles as well as being constituents in maintaining hormonal production and protein metabolism. Once again, our new technology enables us to incorporate these helpful compounds into a basic daily supplement.

The following chart lists the essential super antioxidant compounds and their recommended dosages:

Super Antioxidants Complex	Strength
1. Alpha Lipoic Acid	50 mg
2. Bilberry Powder (*Vaccinium myrtillus*)	25 mg

3. Bioperine®   5 mg
   (Black Pepper Extract)
4. Broccoli Powder   50 mg
   (source of sulforaphane)
5. Cabbage Powder   50 mg
6. Citrus Bioflavonoid Complex   150 mg
   (hesperidin, naringin, flavo-
   noids)
7. Coenzyme Q10 (ubiquinone)   25 mg
8. Fruits & Greens Powder   100 mg
   (apricot, bing cherry, cranberry,
   grapefruit, golden delicious
   apple, Hawaiian pineapple,
   lemon, lime, orange, peach, red
   raspberry, red wine grape, rubini
   berry, strawberry, wild blueberry, broccoli, Brussels sprout,
   cabbage, carrot, celery stalk, Jer-
   sey tomato, kale, rosemary,
   spinach)
9. Glutathione   10 mg
10. Grape-Seed Extract   50 mg
    (*Vitis vinifera L.*)
11. Grape-Skin Extract   25 mg
    (*Vitis vinifera L.*)
12. Green Tea Extract   50 mg
    (*Camellia sinensis*)

13.	Lycopene	1,000 mcg
14.	Mixed Tocotrienol Complex (alpha, delta, gamma)	5 mg
15.	N-acetyl-L-cysteine	50 mg
16.	Para-aminobenzoic acid (PABA)	10 mg
17.	Quercetin	25 mg
18.	Rutin	25 mg
19.	Tomato Powder (source of lycopene)	50 mg
20.	Vitamin E (as natural d-alpha tocopheryl, naturally mixed tocopherols)	5 IU

ESSENTIAL FATTY ACIDS

Finally, your supplement program has to have fat in it. That may sound odd, but when you realize that some 60 to 80 percent of the brain and nervous system are made of fat, then you begin to realize that some fats are actually crucial building blocks for proper health. Now, I am not talking about all fats, because the truth is that there are good fats and bad fats. Most fats in red meats we can definitely live without, but the omega-3 fatty acids found in many types of fish and nuts, such as EPA, DHA, and GLA, are key to all of the systems in our bodies. That is why these are called the essential fatty acids.

DOCOSAHEXAENOIC ACID (DHA) AND EICOSAPENTAENOIC ACID (EPA): We have discussed many times how Genesis 1:29 records that in the green plants and seed-bearing plants of the earth God has given us all the things we need for food. Well, in Genesis 9:2–3 we see that God added fish to this "vegetarian diet." Do you remember that the last meal Jesus ate on earth was fish? Some of the longest-living peoples on earth are big fish eaters. Fish, particularly the cold-water fish like salmon, cod, herring and mackerel, have a protective roll of fat in them that contains something very important to our bodies: the essential fatty acids *docosahexaenoic acid* (DHA) and *eicosapentaenoic acid* (EPA).

As we discussed earlier in chapter 2 about the recent announcement from the American Heart Association, these omega-3 fatty acids are valuable in preventing repeated coronary heart disease events. However, the benefits of these do not stop there; they also affect proper mental and nervous system function as well as positively affecting symptoms of depression, anxiety, attention-deficit hyperactivity disorder (ADHD), age-related memory loss (ARML), dementia, Alzheimer's disease, and some vision problems, among other conditions.

Studies indicate that several conditions associated with aging—such as forgetfulness, dementia, sensory defects, and Alzheimer's disease—may be associated with inadequate amounts of DHA in the diet. DHA is one of the primary structural fatty acids found in the retina of the eye and in the gray matter of the brain (the human brain is between 60 and 80 percent fat, and DHA is the most abundant fat found in it). Because of this it also appears that depression, visual problems, and attention deficit/hyperactivity disorders (ADHD) may also be associated with low DHA levels.

Along with its cousin eicosapentaenoic

acid (EPA), DHA also helps lower cholesterol and triglyceride levels and reduces the stickiness of platelets. This in turn reduces the formation of blood clots. EPA and DHA help decrease arthritic symptoms by regulating chemicals known as *prostaglandin* and *leukotrienes,* which promote inflammation.

Keeping constant levels of omega-3 fatty acids such as DHA and EPA in our systems can reduce the risk of facing many of these diseases. Considering the dramatic increase in these various diseases, doesn't it make sense that we would supplement our diet with fish oil capsules that contain these essential fatty acids?

GAMMA LINOLENIC ACID (GLA): The best source of gamma linolenic acid comes from evening primrose oil. Your body can make GLA, but you have to have a large quantity of vitamins and minerals in your system to do it. Being able to extract it from the evening primrose plant has been a great breakthrough in getting regular doses of this essential omega-6 fatty acid. Oddly enough, evening primrose is a very common plant. It usually grows in dry regions, often beside roadways. Its technical name is *oenothera biennis*.

GLA is very important in fighting inflammation. In my research I have come across more than forty different papers that talk about the role of GLA in decreasing inflammation. Inflammation is directly tied to various illnesses such as heart disease, skin problems, and joint issues. PMS symptoms are reduced by GLA. Neuropathy in diabetics is benefited by GLA. It penetrates the nerves and can actually overcome the pain and numbness associated with neuropathy. It is also important for arthritis, normal wear and tear on the body, osteoarthritis, Crohn's disease, Ileitis, and various forms of colitis. The other thing that GLA does is work directly on the LDL cholesterol—in one study it dropped it about nine percentage points, and for every percentage point dropped of LDL cholesterol, there is a 2 percent decrease in the risk of heart attack.

Did you know many aches and pains are

due to an overly reactive inflammatory system that in many cases just needs to be calmed down? Because science has learned how to derive GLA from the evening primrose plant, we can now take it in a supplement form that is direct and effective in keeping inflammation regulated and protecting us from all of the problems inflammation can cause.

The following chart contains the dosages of these essential fatty acids that I recommend as part of your regular daily supplementation:

Essential Fatty Acids Complex	Strength
1. Evening Primrose Oil (gamma linolenic acid [GLA])	1,000 mg
2. Marine Oils (docosahexaenoic acid [DHA] and eicosapentaenoic acid [EPA] as fish oils)	2,000 mg

BASIC NUTRITIONAL SUPPORT IS A MAJOR KEY TO LONGEVITY AND STAYING HEALTHY

I truly believe that this is what Jesus had in mind in Luke 21 when he said, "Be on guard." Jesus was talking about the health laws in one respect, because he referred to disease. Why was he talking about the health laws? Because under the new covenant those health laws didn't disappear, just as spiritual health still depends upon physical obedience to God's Word. As Exodus 23:25 tells us, disease is taken away from us as His blessing is on what we eat. There are some very specific things we should be doing to take care of our bodies and one of them is replacing the elements that are missing or dwindling in our food supply.

Would you do something simple if you knew it had great benefits for your health? Starting a daily supplement program to put these seven essential complexes into your daily diet may well be one of the easiest steps you can take. It may require some effort to break through the confusion at first, but once you have your system down, it is easier to make it a part of your daily routine than adding exercise or changing what you eat. Don't misunderstand; you still may need to do both of these other things, but starting a daily supplement program is by far the easiest of the three!

Just in case you are still wondering what the need for these seven complexes is, go to *www.abundantnutrition.com/bns.html#* and click on the box that reads "How Basic Nutrient Support Can Address Your Health Concerns." The chart there will show you how each of these seven complexes addresses the health concerns we discussed in chapter 2.

God really does want to make it easy for you. I hope this information has encouraged you to renew your interest in taking basic nutrient supplements daily or, if you are already doing so, to compare your current supplement program with some of the new technology mentioned in this chapter. Technology has come a long way in providing various beneficial compounds in supplement form from the plant and animal kingdom God created for our benefit.

God has called us to be the "light of the world" in these last days. To be this light, we need to be free of pain and disease in our bodies so that we have the strength to reach out to others. This is all part of God's plan for our lives. He wants us to walk in health.

Chapter 4

YOUR DAILY WALK ON THE PATHWAY TO HEALING AND DIVINE HEALTH

Chapter 4

YOUR DAILY WALK ON THE PATHWAY TO HEALING AND DIVINE HEALTH

"Be on your guard and be careful that you are not led astray.... There will be ... pestilences (plagues, malignant and contagious or infectious epidemic diseases, deadly and devastating).... Now when these things begin to occur, look up and lift up your heads, because your redemption (deliverance) is drawing near" (Luke 21:8, 11, 28 AMP).

As we face these pestilences of the last days, it is good to know that God is on our side and is providing us with wisdom to counteract them. As He blesses our food and nutritional intake, we will significantly reduce our chances of facing these pestilences, and we can be an example of His goodness and grace to others. Before finishing this discussion of vitamins and nutritional supplements, I do want to offer a few more words of advice that I hope you find helpful.

SOME BASIC GUIDELINES FOR TAKING SUPPLEMENTS

"SANDWICH" SUPPLEMENTS INTO YOUR MEALS: Your nutritional supplement program should include a morning and evening "packet" to take or may include supplements to be taken three times a day. As some ingredients interfere with the absorption of other ingredients, it is best to separate these out into A.M. and P.M. dosages to maximize their absorption.

The easiest way I have found to take these is during mealtimes. It can be very hard on your stomach to take a handful of pills, tablets, and capsules and simply chase them down with a glassful of water. In fact, the unpleasantness of swallowing all of these at once has convinced more than a few people that taking supplements is not for them!

This is why I have always suggested sandwiching supplements into meals. Eat a small amount of food, take a supplement; eat a little more, take another; continuing until you have taken them all. This eliminates the unpleasantness of swallowing them all at once as well as most of the aftertaste they may leave and the nausea sometimes associated with taking supplements on an empty stomach. It also aids in the absorption of the nutrients in them and stops the "vitamin burps" often associated with taking marine oil capsules.

Another way Linda and I take supplements is with 100 percent Concord grape juice. We generally drink six ounces of this juice every morning with our meal because of the bioflavonoids and other benefits it has, and the tartness of it seems to cut the "vitamin taste."

If these suggestions don't work for you, you can also grind supplements up in a blender and drink them in a fruit smoothie. This a rather labor-intensive solution, but some patients we have suggested it to find it a great method to help them get their nutritional supplements in regularly.

MORE IS NOT ALWAYS BETTER: I know I have made this point before, but it bears repeating. You need to be careful not to take more than the dosages I have recommended if you can help it. Now, more of some things can be helpful, but too much of many things can also be harmful in the long run. We must remember that vitamins, minerals, extracts, and the like are chemicals and often act as drugs in our system. Just as swallowing the entire bottle of antibiotics on the first day you receive the prescription is a foolish thing to do, so taking too much of any one supplement every day can also be harmful.

The idea is to maintain a safe and helpful level of these nutrients in our bloodstream over time. Too much of some can have negative side effects, especially if we maintain concentrations of them that are too high for too long. If you feel that you need more of one element to address a specific concern, check with your physician first to see what effect it will have when combined with other supplements or medications you may be taking on a regular or short-term basis.

READ THE LABELS AND FOLLOW DIRECTIONS: Though this seems very basic, it cannot go without saying. Read the labels to see what is in the tablets or capsules you are taking, especially if you are taking more than one multivitamin, mineral, or other supplement. They may be giving you too much of something or two different ingredients that fight each other for absorption, such as iron and zinc do. Also follow the directions on how to take them to optimize absorption and avoid unpleasant side effects.

COMBINE YOUR DAILY NUTRITIONAL SUPPORT WITH DAILY SPIRITUAL SUPPORT AND SOUND MEDICAL ADVICE SPECIFIC TO YOUR NEEDS

You have to act on the truths you have received. Take the following steps to make sure you receive God's unique plan for healthy living or pathway to healing for you.

Step 1: Consult with a physician or reliable medical professional. Make sure you have regular checkups to catch potential problems early, when they are easiest to treat and correct. Many say that they don't need to go to doctors because they are doing all the things they need to do on their own to maintain their health. I believe this can be fear speaking more than wisdom. Having regular checkups not only keeps you from unnecessary worrying about your health, but it also gives you the chance to discuss things with your health professional that you would not normally have the opportunity to do.

Consultation with a physician or a competent medical professional can give you information about your nutritional intake that is vital. Make sure you discuss with your health advisor all of the different things that you may be taking to ensure that there are no conflicts. This person may even be able to suggest packaged supplement programs that contain all or most of what you need, which can make taking all the supplements you need every day even easier.

Step 2: Pray with understanding. Seek God in prayer and ask Him to reveal to you and to your doctor the best steps in the natural that you can take to proceed down your pathway to maintaining your health or receiving your healing.

If you are not sure how to pray, you can begin by praying a prayer like this:

> *Lord, in Jesus' name, show me the pathway that will lead to maintaining my health (or receiving my healing) by getting the nutrients my body needs. Show me that unique pathway you have designed for me, because I know I am fearfully and wonderfully made. You are my Creator as well as my Father, and you know me better than anyone because you made me. Deliver me from being stubborn and having my mind made up in my own ignorance or arrogance. Show me your way clearly. I am open to however you want to keep me*

healthy (or heal me) and however you would like to work in my life.

Thank you for your promises of healing in the Bible and all of the examples of the different pathways to healing you have shown us in your Word. I know you have a special path for me, and I will rely on you to reveal it to me. Thank you for leading me to it, Lord. Amen.

While much of the advice I have offered in this pocket book is natural, do not neglect your daily spiritual needs. Make sure to "supplement" what you take into your mind every day with solid doses of God's Word and prayer. Only then can God lead you into fullness and the abundant life He has promised you in every area.

Step 3: Ask the Holy Spirit to guide you to truth. We have given you a great deal of information about the compounds you can take to help your physical body, and it is quite possible that your medical advisor will give you some other options. By referring to the information in this book, you can bring up the discussion of what nutritional supplements would be best for you. Approach your health professional by asking if he or she would be willing to work with you in developing a nutritional supplement program or if they have such programs that they already endorse.

I strongly encourage you to explore all the aspects of the vitamins and supplements that I have described to you in this book—the pathways that God has created to strengthen and guard your health. You need to pray in faith that God will give you the wisdom you need in order to discern the one pathway He has provided that is best for you. It is good to know that in James 1:5 we have God's promise about receiving this wisdom: "If any of you lack wisdom, let him ask of God, that giveth to all men liberally, and upbraideth not; and it shall be given him." Allow the Holy Spirit to guide you into all truth.

Step 4: Maintain proper and healthy nutrition. Exercise your body and mind to stay fit. I want to emphasize again that while starting a nutritional supplement program is an easy

first step, it is not the only step. I encourage
you to adopt as many principles of a healthy
diet as possible and to incorporate into it the
foods, herbs, and natural supplements we have
discussed in this book. Do not neglect exercise. Not only is it good for us in general,
studies have shown that regular exercise can
reduce many of the symptoms of aging. Other
studies have shown that those who continue
to challenge themselves intellectually maintain
healthier mental faculties. Establish an active
life for an active mind.

*Step 5: Stand firm in God's pathway to heal-
ing for you.* Refuse to be discouraged or
defeated. Be aggressive in prayer and in faith,
claiming your health and healing in Jesus
Christ.

There are nineteen individually recorded
healings in the Gospels, and each is unique. I
believe these are all recorded in the Scriptures
to show us the principle that God uses different pathways of healing for different people.
When I realized this, it completely changed
the way I practiced medicine. It is incredible

how, when I started praying and asking God to show *me,* as a doctor, His pathway to healing for each of my patients, I began to see more and more clearly His design for helping each person. Through prayer, faith, knowledge, and wisdom, God can show you His pathway to maintaining health or receiving healing.

If we are just open to that, God will work miracles. It may be instantaneous, or it may be a process or treatment that takes some time. It may involve certain medicines or even surgery. It may also be a pathway that is relatively uneventful as we stay healthy and have regular checkups that find no disease. Thank God that we have a way to pray for our healing, but thank God as well that we can take precautions before we are sick to avoid the need for healing. Both give us tremendous hope.

Hebrews 11:1 says that faith gives substance to those things that we hope for. If you don't have anything to hope for, how will faith give substance to it? You must have hope, and that comes when you know that God has a pathway to health or healing for you. That is a promise you can pray for, have faith in, and hold on to. Thank God for His promises!

These are principles you need to apply in all areas of your life, but you can also specifically apply them with regard to your physical health. You need to seek God about the areas you are concerned with and get His answers. See a physician to get the right information so that you know how to more specifically pray. God knows your needs and the best way for you to receive your healing and maintain your health. Hang onto the hope of His promises and He will show you His plan for healthy living that is designed especially for you.

ENDNOTES

Chapter 1

1. J. R. Herbert, J. Barone, et al., "Natural-Killer Cell Activity in a Longitudinal Dietary Fat Intervention Trial," *Clinical Immunology and Immunopathology* 54, no. 1 (January 1990): 103–16; and J. Barone, J. R. Herbert, and M. M. Reddy, "Dietary Fat and Natural-Killer Cell Activity," *American Journal of Clinical Nutrition* 50, no. 4 (October 1989): 861–67.

Chapter 2

1. Walter C. Willet and Meir J. Stampfer, "Rebuilding the Food Pyramid," *Scientific American*, vol. 228, no. 1, (January 2003): 64–71; and Geoffrey Cowley, "A Better Way to Eat," *Newsweek,* vol. 141, no. 3 (20 January 2003): 46–64.

2. Robert H. Fletcherm, M.D., MSc; and Kathleen M. Farfield, M.D., DrPH; "Vitamins for

Chronic Disease Prevention in Adults: Clinical Applications," *The Journal of the American Medical Association* 287, no. 23 (19 June 2002): 3129.

3. Mitchel L. Zoler, "*AHA* Endorses Fish Oil Supplements" (15 January 2003): 1, 5.

4. Ranjit Kumar Chandra, M.D., "Effect of Vitamin and Trace-Element Supplementation on Cognitive Function in Elderly Subjects," *Nutrition* 17, no. 9 (September 2001): 709–12.

5. Also reported in *Nutrition* magazine.

6. Paul Zimmer, Cutberto Garza, et al., "Postpartum Maternal Blood Helper T (CD3+CD4+) and Cytotoxic T (CD3+CD8+) Cells: Correlations With Iron Status, Parity, Supplement Use, and Lactation Status 1–3J," *American Journal of Clinical Nutrition* 67, no. 5 (May 1998): 897–904.

7. J. Gruenwald, H. J. Graubaum, and A. Harde, "Effect of a Probiotic Multivitamin Compound on Stress and Exhaustion," *Advances in Therapy* 19, no. 3 (May-June 2002): 141–50.

8. Fletcherm and Farfield, "Vitamins for Chronic Disease Prevention in Adults: Clinical Applications," 3127.

9. *Prevention* magazine, *Complete Book of Vita-*

mins and Minerals (N.Y.: Random House, 1992).

Chapter 3

1. Whole Health M.D., L.L.C., "Vitamin D," online at *www.wholehealthmd.com/refshelf/substances_view/0,1525,905,00.html*, © 2000. Accessed: 10 March 2003.
2. "Vitamin E—Miracle or Myth?" *Nutrition Reviews* 32, no. 0, supplement 1 (July 1974): 35–36.
3. Whole Health M.D., L.L.C., "Trace Minerals," online at *www.wholehealthmd.com/refshelf/substances_view/0,1525,10061,00.html*, © 2000. Updated: 2 March 2003. Accessed: 5 March 2003.
4. Ibid.
5. Supplement Watch, "Papain," online at *www.supplementwatch.com/supatoz/supplement.asp?supplementId 49*. Accessed: 3 March 2003.
6. Whole Health MD, "Glutathione," online at: *www.wholehealthmd.com/refshelf/substances_view/0,1525,854,00.html*, © 2000. Updated: 17 February 2003. Accessed: 5 March 2003.

REGINALD B. CHERRY, M.D.—A MEDICAL DOCTOR'S TESTIMONY

The first six years of my life were lived in the dusty rural town of Mansfield, in the Ouachita Mountains of western Arkansas. In those childhood years, I had one seemingly impossible dream—to become a doctor!

Through God's grace, I graduated from Baylor University and the University of Texas Medical School. Throughout those years, I felt God tug on my heart a number of times, especially through Billy Graham as I heard him preach on TV. But I never surrendered my life to Jesus Christ.

In those early days of practicing medicine, I met Dr. Kenneth Cooper and became trained in the field of preventive medicine. In the mid-seventies I moved to Houston and established a medical practice for preventive medicine. Sadly, at that time money became a driving force in my life.

Nevertheless, God was looking out for me. He brought into our clinic a nurse who became a Spirit-filled Christian, and she began praying for me. In fact, she had her whole church praying for me!

In my search for fulfillment and meaning in life, I called out to God one night in late November 1979 and prayed, *Jesus, I give you everything I own. I'm sorry for the life I've lived. I want to live for you the rest of my days. I give you my life.* A doctor had been born again, and that beautiful nurse, Linda, who had prayed for me and shared Jesus with me, is now my wife!

Not only did Jesus transform my life but He also transformed my medical practice. God spoke to me and said, in effect, "I want you to establish a Christian clinic. From now on when you practice medicine, you will be *ministering* to patients." I began to pray for patients seeking God's pathway to healing in the supernatural realm as well as in the natural realm.

Over the years we have witnessed how God has miraculously used both supernatural and natural pathways to heal our patients and to demonstrate His marvelous healing and saving power.

I know what God has done in my life, and I know what God has done in the lives of our patients. He can do the same in your life—in fact, He has a unique pathway to healing for you! He is the Lord that heals you (see Exodus 15:26). By His stripes you were healed (see Isaiah 53:5).

Linda and I are standing with you as you seek God's pathway to healing through vitamins and nutritional supplements and as you walk in His pathway to total healing for your life.

If you do not know Jesus Christ as your personal Lord and Savior, I invite you to pray the following prayer and ask Jesus to come into your life:

Lord Jesus, I invite you into my life as my Lord and Savior. I repent of my past sins. I ask you to forgive me. Thank you for shedding your blood on the cross to cleanse me from my sin and to heal me. I receive your gift of everlasting life and surrender all to you. Thank you, Jesus, for saving me. Amen.

ABOUT THE AUTHOR

Reginald B. Cherry, M.D., did his premed at Baylor University, graduated from the University of Texas Medical School, and has practiced diagnostic and preventive medicine for more than twenty-five years. His work in medicine has been recognized and honored by the city of Houston and by President George W. Bush when he was governor of Texas.

Dr. Cherry and his wife, Linda, a clinical nurse who has worked with Dr. Cherry and his patients during the past two-and-a-half decades, now host the popular television program *The Doctor and the Word*, which has a potential weekly viewing audience of 90 million homes. They also publish a monthly medical newsletter and produce topical audiocassette teachings, pocket books such as this one, and booklets. Dr. Cherry is author of the bestselling books *The Doctor and the Word*, *The Bible Cure*, and *Healing Prayer*.

RESOURCES AVAILABLE FROM REGINALD B. CHERRY MINISTRIES, INC.

BOOKS

Prayers That Heal: Faith-Building Prayers When You Need a Miracle

Combining the wisdom of over twenty-five years of medical practice and the revelation of God's Word, Dr. Cherry provides the knowledge you need to pray effectively against diabetes, cancer, heart disease, eye problems, hypoglycemia, and fifteen other common afflictions that rob you of your health.

Healing Prayer

A fascinating in-depth look at a vital link between spiritual and physical healing. Dr. Cherry presents actual case histories of people healed through prayer, plus the latest information on herbs, vitamins, and supplements that promote vibrant health. This is sound information you need to keep you healthy—mind, soul, and body.

God's Pathway to Healing: Bone Health

Bone mass loss and osteoporosis affect more than 34 million Americans today, and statistics indicate that these numbers will continue to grow dramatically in the decades to come. Though bone disease affects four times the number of women as men, the men who suffer from its complications are often twice as likely to die from them as are women. None of us has room to ignore this debilitating ailment; we all need to do what we can now to either prevent or reverse its effects. In this pocket book, Dr. Cherry shares with readers the things they can do, no matter their age, to strengthen bones and immensely reduce the risks of bone mass loss that results in fractures that can rob us of the quality of life God promised us, if not take life from us altogether. This is a book for all ages and both sexes, as building strong bones is an issue all of us need to address.

God's Pathway to Healing: Diabetes

Diabetes is reaching epidemic proportions as 17 million Americans now face the disease—more than one-third of them not even aware that they have it—and another one million a year will develop it. Some statistics suggest that by the year 2025, one in four Americans will have diabetes. The severe complications of diabetes also give us reason for concern, since it more than triples the risk of death for young adults who acquire it. However, God has a pathway both for prevention and healing of this proliferating disease. In this pocket book, Dr. Cherry outlines the lifestyle changes to prevent and control diabetes as well as the best medications and natural alternatives for reducing its threat to our overall health. This is a book no one can afford to miss, as diabetes most likely affects at least one person you know.

God's Pathway to Healing: Digestion

Dr. Cherry discusses keys to a naturally healthy digestive system, including better digestion and absorption of food, proper elimination of waste, and the place of "good" bacteria. He points readers toward better eating habits and natural nutritional supplements to improve digestion.

God's Pathway to Healing: Heart

Heart disease kills twice as many people as all the forms of cancer combined, and more than half of the body of Christ dies of coronary artery or cardiovascular diseases. However, there are things that you can do to keep yourself free of heart disease. An incredible wealth of research in recent years has been done on natural extracts and foods that will feed this muscle and keep it strong and healthy. When these nutrients are combined with faith, prayer, and God's Word, you will find yourself quickly on God's pathway to healing and a healthy heart.

God's Pathway to Healing: Herbs That Heal

Learn the truth about common herbal remedies and discover the possible side effects of each. Discover which herbs can help treat symptoms of insomnia, arthritis, heart problems, asthma, and many other conditions. Read this book and see if herbs are part of God's pathway to healing for you.

God's Pathway to Healing: Joints and Arthritis

Dr. Cherry says painful joints and arthritis do not have to be part of aging. Recent medical breakthroughs show that natural substances can relieve pain and inflammation and slow or prevent cartilage loss.

God's Pathway to Healing: The Immune System

We are truly fearfully and wonderfully made, and part of that amazing creation is something God built into us to keep us all healthy for life: our immune system. In this insightful pocket book, Dr. Cherry explains the basic function of this "everyday miracle," which even medical science has yet to fully understand, as well as steps we can take to keep it strong and balanced so that it will do what God designed it to do: "Keep sickness from the midst of us" (Exodus 23:25).

God's Pathway to Healing: Memory and Mental Acuity

As the baby-boomer generation ages, we are facing more problems with mental function than ever before. Whether it is because of age-related memory loss or poor nutrition or pollutants we take in that affect the way we think and concentrate, people of all ages need new information about how to keep their minds healthy and strong. In this pocket book, Dr. Cherry addresses these concerns in a straightforward and easy-to-understand manner that can help people facing such ailments such as depression, attention-deficit hyperactivity disorder (ADHD), migraine headaches, Alzheimer's disease, and many other concerns associated with our brain's function. This book may well be God's key for you to a healthy memory and sharp, focused mind.

God's Pathway to Healing: Menopause

This pocket book is full of helpful advice for women who are going through what potentially can be a very stressful time of life. Find out what foods, supplements, and steps lead to a pathway to healing for menopause and perimenopause.

God's Pathway to Healing: Prostate

This pocket book is packed with enlightening insights for men who are searching for ways to prevent prostate cancer or who have actually been diagnosed with the disease. Discover how foods, plant-derived natural supplements, and a change in diet can be incorporated into your life to help you find a pathway to healing for prostate disease.

God's Pathway to Healing: Vision

Macular degeneration, cataracts, vision degeneration due to complications of diabetes, and other eye conditions can be slowed or prevented. Dr. Cherry discusses herbs and nutritional changes people can make to keep their vision strong.

God's Pathway to Healing: Vitamins and Supplements

With the growing number of supplements and multivitamins on the market today, it is difficult to know what to take and when and how to avoid taking more than is needed or in combinations that could be harmful. This easy-to-follow pocket book is a tremendous reference for anyone desiring to stay healthy in this age when new diseases seem to be discovered more often than ever before. This book could be the key to discovering the miraculous power God has unlocked through natural extracts and nutritional supplements to keep us healthy to the end of our days.

Dr. Cherry's Little Instruction Book for Health and Healing

Easy-to-read information about healthy habits, natural remedies, and nutritional guidance, along with biblical principles for supernatural healing; prayers and Scripture make this a great reminder that God's desire is that His people be healthy. This is a helpful small volume for readers familiar with Dr. Cherry's work and a great introduction for those who are new to his ministry.

The Bible Cure (now in paperback)

Dr. Cherry presents hidden truths in the Bible taken from ancient dietary health laws, how Jesus anointed with natural substances to heal, and how to activate faith through prayer for health and healing. This book validates scientific medical research by using it to reveal God's original health plan.

The Doctor and the Word (now in paperback)

Dr. Cherry introduces the idea of how God has a pathway to healing for everyone. Jesus healed instantaneously as well as through a process. Discover how the manifestation of your healing can come about by seeking His ways.

Dr. Cherry's Study Guides, Volume 2
(a bound volume)

Receive thirty valuable resource study guides from topics Dr. Cherry has taught on the Trinity Broadcasting Network (TBN) program *The Doctor and the Word*.

Basic Nutrient Support

Dr. Cherry has developed a daily nutrient supplement that is the simplest to take and yet the most complete supplement available today. Protect your body daily with more than sixty natural substances that fight cancer, heart disease, and many other problems. Call Natural Alternatives at (800) 339-5952 to place your order. Please mention service code "BN30" when ordering. (Or order through the company's Web site: *www.Abundant Nutrition.com.*)

Other Nutrient Support Programs to Address Specific Health Concerns

In addition to his Basic Nutrient Support program, Dr. Cherry has also developed daily nutrient supplements to address other health concerns. Here is a brief list of some that are now available:

- Blood Sugar Program
- Cardiovascular Support
- Digestion Support
- Immunity Support
- Memory and Mental Support
- Menopause Support
- Prostate Support
- Stress Support
- Sleep Support
- Weight Management Program

Call Natural Alternatives at (800) 339-5952 or visit *www.AbundantNutrition.com* to get the full list of supplement programs or to place your order. Please mention service code "BN30" when ordering.

Reginald B. Cherry Ministries, Inc.
P.O. Box 27711
Houston, TX 77227-7711
1-888-DRCHERRY

BECOME A PATHWAY TO HEALING PARTNER

We invite you to become a pathway partner. We ask you to stand with us in prayer and financial support as we provide new programs, resources, books, pocket books, and a unique, one-of-a-kind monthly newsletter.

Our monthly Pathway to Healing Partner newsletter sorts through the confusion about health and healing. In it, Dr. Cherry shares sensible biblical and medical steps you can take to get well and stay well. Every issue points you to your pathway to healing. Writing from a Christian physician's Bible-based point of view, Dr. Cherry talks about nutrition and health, how to pray for specific diseases, updates on the latest medical research, Linda's own recipes for healthy eating, and questions and answers concerning issues you need to know about.

In addition, we'll provide you with Dr. Cherry and Linda's ministry calendar, broadcast schedule, resources for better living, and special monthly offers.

This newsletter is available to you as you partner with the Cherrys through prayer and monthly financial support to help expand this God-given ministry. Pray today about responding with a monthly contribution. Call us or write to the following address to find out how you can receive this valuable information.

Become a pathway partner today
by writing:
Reginald B. Cherry Ministries, Inc.
P.O. Box 27711
Houston, TX 77227-7711
Visit our Web site:
www.drcherry.org
1-888-DRCHERRY

REGINALD B. CHERRY, M.D.,
did his premed at Baylor
University and graduated
from the University of Texas
Medical School. He practiced
diagnostic and preventive
medicine in Houston, Texas,
for 25 years. Dr. Cherry and
his wife, Linda, a clinical
nurse, host the popular television program *The Doctor
and the Word*. He speaks
nationwide, and his books
The Doctor and the Word and
The Bible Cure are bestsellers.

VITAMINS AND SUPPLEMENTS

taken daily
provide nutritional protection and
can help those facing specific
health issues. Most Americans do
not get sufficient vitamins and
nutrients from the foods they eat,
and these deficiencies have been
linked with chronic illness and
disease. In this easy-to-use guide,
Dr. Cherry explains what God
has provided naturally for opti-
mum health, which nutritional
supplements to take, and how to
get the most value from them.
Start on God's Pathway to Healing
and prevention of disease today.

www.bethanyhouse.com

US $6.99   Health

ISBN 0-7642-2813-7

BETHANY HOUSE
PUBLISHERS

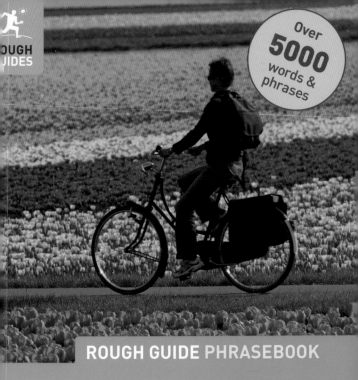

ROUGH GUIDE PHRASEBOOK

DUTCH

Free audio download